ROLLER COASTER SCIENCE

Other Titles of Interest from Wiley

Science for Every Kid series

Janice VanCleave's Astronomy for Every Kid
Janice VanCleave's Biology for Every Kid
Janice VanCleave's Chemistry for Every Kid
Janice VanCleave's Earth Science for Every Kid
Janice VanCleave's Geography for Every Kid
Janice VanCleave's Math for Every Kid
Janice VanCleave's Physics for Every Kid

Spectacular Science Projects series

Janice VanCleave's Animals
Janice VanCleave's Earthquakes
Janice VanCleave's Gravity
Janice VanCleave's Machines
Janice VanCleave's Magnets
Janice VanCleave's Microscopes and Magnifying Lenses
Janice VanCleave's Molecules

Projects for a Healthy Planet, Shar Levine and Allison Grafton

The Complete Handbook of Science Fair Projects,
Julianne Bochinski

The Thomas Edison Book of Easy and Incredible Experiments,
The Thomas Alva Edison Foundation

The Ocean Book, Center for Marine Conservation

The Earth Science Book, Dinah Zike

Flying Start Science series

Action
Flight
Light
Pattern
Structure
Water

David Suzuki's Looking At series

Looking at the Body
Looking at the Environment
Looking at Insects
Looking at Plants
Looking at Senses
Looking at Weather

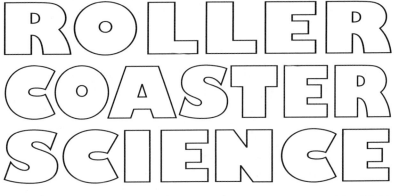

ROLLER COASTER SCIENCE

50 Wet, Wacky, Wild, Dizzy Experiments about Things Kids Like Best

Jim Wiese

John Wiley & Sons, Inc.

New York • Chichester • Brisbane • Toronto • Singapore

Library of Congress Cataloging-in-Publication Data:

Wiese, Jim.
    Roller coaster science : 50 wet, wacky, wild, dizzy experiments
about things kids like best / Jim Wiese.
        p.   cm.
    Includes index.
Summary: Describes the science behind such amusements as roller coasters, swings, bumper cars, hot dogs, curve balls, and more. Includes easy experiments to do.
    ISBN 0-471-59404-0 (pbk.)
    1. Science—Experiments—Juvenile literature   2. Science—Miscellanea—
Juvenile literature. [1. Science—Experiments. 2. Experiments.]   I. Title
Q 164.W533 1994
507.8—dc20   93-19851

Printed in the United States of America
10 9 8 7 6 5 4

For Barbara, Matthew, and Elizabeth,
who help to make my life fun

ACKNOWLEDGMENTS

I would like to give special thanks to Karen Luke for her word processing expertise and to Elaine Nutbrown for providing some of the graphics used in this book. They both helped to turn my rough ideas into a finished product. I would also like to thank all the teachers who have shared ideas with me over the years, especially Don Rathgen at Foothills High School in Pleasanton, California. Don's collaboration in starting a local Amusement Park Physics program was an early step for me in trying to make science fun.

It goes without saying that I greatly appreciate John Wiley & Sons' confidence in me. Without their support, this book would not have been possible.

CONTENTS

2 Round and Round We Go

4 Excitement on the Midway

INTRODUCTION

What comes to mind when you think about playgrounds and amusement parks, toys and cotton candy? Chances are you think of fun. But even in fun there is science. Science is all around us if we will only take the time to look for it. There is more to swings, roller coasters, and other fun activities than first meets the eye. So be prepared to look at them in a new way in *Roller Coaster Science.*

Before You Start

This book is full of information and simple science experiments that will help you to discover more about how things work and why things happen in the world around you. The book is divided into sections based on general topic areas: playgrounds, amusement parks, recreational activities, games, and fun foods. Words in **bold** type are defined in the Glossary at tthe back of the book.

You will be able to find most of the equipment you need for the experiments around your house, at a neighborhood playground, or possibly at a local amusement park. You do not need expensive equipment to be a good scientist. You need only to have an open mind that asks questions and looks for answers. After all, the basis of good science is asking good questions and finding the best answers.

How to Be a Good Scientist

- Collect all the equipment you will need before you start the activity or experiment.
- If possible, keep a notebook. Write down what you do in your experiment and what happens
- Read through the instructions once completely before you start the activity or experiment.
- Follow the instructions carefully. Do not attempt to do yourself any steps that require the help of an adult.
- If your experiment does not work properly the first time, try again or try doing it in a slightly different way. In real life, experiments don't always work out perfectly the first time.

Increasing Your Understanding

- Make small changes in the design of the equipment to see if the results are the same–but change only one thing at a time.
- Make up an experiment or activity to test your own ideas about how things work.
- Look at the things around you for examples of the scientific principles that you have learned.
- Do not worry if at first you do not understand the things around you. There are always new things to discover. Remember that many of the most famous discoveries were made by accident.

A Word of Warning

Some science experiments can be dangerous. Ask an adult to help you when the experiment calls for adult help, especially those that involve knives or other sharp instruments. Don't forget to ask your parents' permission to use household items, and put away your equipment when you have finished. Good scientists are careful and avoid accidents.

What Goes Up

Playground Activities

The rides at a playground are a great place
to learn basic physics. But before you turn
to another chapter because you think physics
is too hard and you can't understand it, drop this
book. You just experimented with gravity. Gravity,
a force we all know about, is basic to the study
of physics. See, physics lesson number one wasn't
so hard. Read on and see what other things
you can learn.

DOWNHILL RACER
THE SLIDE

Go to a school or neighborhood playground. Do the following experiments on a slide.

ACTIVITY 1
THE STRAIGHT SLIDE

Procedure

1. Ride the slide from the very top all the way to the bottom.
2. Next, slide halfway down, then stop yourself by carefully grabbing the sides. Now let yourself slide the rest of the way down. Make sure you don't do any extra pushing.
3. How does your final speed in the first case compare to your final speed in the second?

MORE FUN STUFF TO DO

How Far Can It Go?

Try the same experiment with a smooth ball. First, start the ball at the top of the slide. See how far it rolls when it gets to the end of the slide. Next, start the ball at the middle of the slide. Compare the distance the ball traveled when it started near the middle to the distance it traveled when it started near the top of the slide. Are the distances the same?

THE CURVED SLIDE

Some playgrounds have slides that make a twisting curve on the way to the bottom. If you have a slide like that, try the next investigations as well.

Procedure

1. Go to the top of the straight slide with a marble or small ball.
2. Place the marble or ball so that it will roll down the middle of the slide. Let it go and watch what happens. Does the marble stay in the middle of the slide?
3. Do the same thing on the curved slide. What happens to the marble this time? Does it stay in the middle of the slide or move to one side?

   Ride the slides yourself. Do you go faster or slower on the curved slide? Do you move to the inside or the outside of the slide as you go down?

Explanation

The slide provides a perfect illustration of the **law of conservation of energy.** This law states that energy can change from one form to another but cannot be created or destroyed.

At the top of the slide, you have a type of energy called **potential energy** (PE), which is stored energy that can be used later. When you start down the slide, your movement comes from another type of energy, **kinetic energy** (KE), which is energy that is being used, the energy caused by motion.

Get Busy, Get Dizzy

Try to go down the curved slide two or three times in a row. How do you feel? Do you get dizzy?

But where does kinetic energy come from? The law of conservation of energy states that energy can't be created from nothing, so it has to come from somewhere else. Kinetic energy comes from changing some of the potential energy into kinetic energy. The higher the slide, the more potential (stored) energy is converted into kinetic energy or motion. At the bottom of the slide, all the potential energy is changed into kinetic energy and so you go the fastest. The farther you slide, the faster you go.

The diagrams on the next page show the conversion of potential energy (PE) into kinetic energy (KE) during a slide ride. Potential energy is converted into kinetic energy, but the total energy (TE) remains the same. That's the law of conservation of energy.

On a curved slide, **centripetal force** comes into play. This is the force that causes an object to move in a circle. It literally means the "center-seeking" force. Gravity makes you go down the slide in a straight line, but because the slide curves, centripetal force makes you slide along the curve. You think you are being thrown to the outer edge of the slide, but gravity is just trying to make you go straight on a curved slide. (See "Spin Yourself Silly: The Merry-Go-Round," page 19, for another example of centripetal force.)

The ball or marble will behave in the same way. It will move faster if it is started near the top of the slide, and it will move to the outside edge of the curved slide.

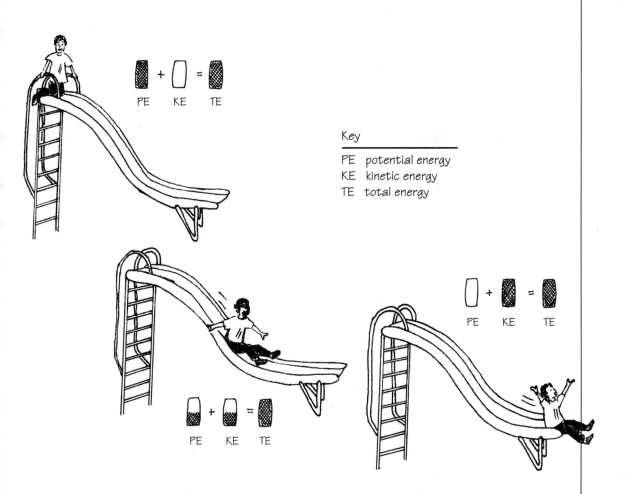

Key

PE   potential energy
KE   kinetic energy
TE   total energy

If you go down a curved slide many times, you may feel sick or dizzy. That's because the inner ear, which is responsible for balance, gets messed up by spinning around in a circle. After a short time it returns to normal.

❖ ACTIVITY 3

FRICTION ON THE SLIDE

Try this next experiment on the slide as well.

Procedure

1. Ride the slide from the top to the bottom.
2. Ride the slide from the top to the bottom again, but this time ride on a piece of waxed paper or a nylon jacket.
3. Which ride was faster?

Explanation

Friction is a force that works in the opposite direction to an object that is moving along a surface. Friction can come in many forms, but it always resists motion. The amount of friction depends mainly on the materials involved. Waxed paper and a nylon jacket help to reduce friction. Can you think of any other way that you could decrease friction?

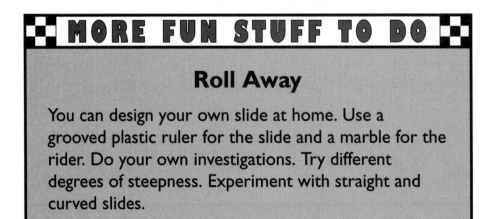

◼ MORE FUN STUFF TO DO ◼

Roll Away

You can design your own slide at home. Use a grooved plastic ruler for the slide and a marble for the rider. Do your own investigations. Try different degrees of steepness. Experiment with straight and curved slides.

UP, UP, AND AWAY
THE SWINGS

ACTIVITY 1
PENDULUM ACTION

The swing is an example of a **pendulum**, a simple
device in which an object (like a swing seat) is suspended
by a rope, chain, or string from a central pivot point. Go
to a local park or playground and try the following
activities to learn about pendulums and swings. You'll
need to take several friends and a stopwatch with you.
Find out what each person weighs before you go. **Weight**
is the force with which an object is pulled toward earth
by gravity. Weight is measured in pounds or kilograms.

Procedure

1. Find a tall swing (one with a flat seat is best).
2. Let the swing hang straight down. Draw a line on
   the ground about 6 feet (2 m) behind the swing seat.
   This is the release mark.
3. Let one friend sit in the swing. Have two others, one
   on each side of the swing, pull the swing back until
   the swing seat is over the release mark.
4. When the timer says "go," the two friends release
   the swing.
5. The timer records how long it takes for the swing to
   go back and forth five complete times (that is, to go
   forward and back to the starting point). The time
   needed for a pendulum to complete one cycle of
   motion is called the **period.**
6. The rider must not shift around on the seat of the
   swing or "pump" the swing.

7 Have each friend take a turn in the swing.

8 Does the weight of the swinging person have any effect on the time it takes the swing to make five complete periods? In other words, does **mass** (properties that cause an object to have weight due to gravity) affect the period of a pendulum?

♦ ACTIVITY 2
RELEASE POINT

Whoever weighs least gets to do the next experiment.

Procedure

1 Let the swing hang straight down again. Draw several lines on the ground behind the swing seat— one at 3 feet (1 m), one at 6 feet (2 m), and one at 9 feet (3 m). These are the release marks.

2 With the lightest person in the swing, have two others pull the swing back to the first release mark.

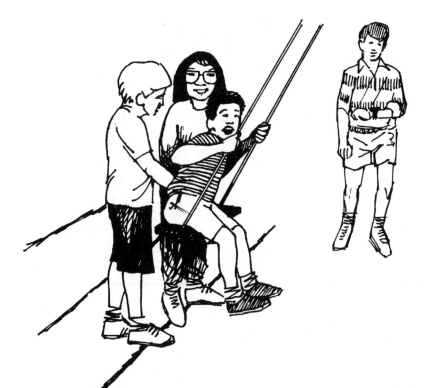

3   When the timer says "go," the two release the swing.

4   The timer records the time for five complete periods as before.

5   Repeat the activity for the other two release marks.

6   Does the release point affect the pendulum's period?

ACTIVITY 3

HOW LONG IS YOUR CHAIN?

You will need a park or playground that has several sets of swings with different lengths of chain to conduct the following investigation.

Procedure

1   Use the person who weighs least as the swinger and a 6-foot (2-m) release point.

2   The timer records the period for the swing the same as in the two previous activities.

3   Repeat the experiment on each swing that has a different length of chain.

4   Does the length of the chain have an effect on the period of the pendulum swing?

5   Let several friends of different weights ride swings with different lengths of chain at the same time. Can you predict which friend will take the longest time to make five complete periods?

Explanation

When it isn't pumped, the swing acts just like a pendulum. That's because it is a pendulum. The only thing that will affect the pendulum's period (the time it

e length of the
...s it. To learn
, Daydream: A
.2).

■ A.....   r

GET PUMPED

How does pumping a swing work? Once you get a swing
started, how does pumping make you go higher? Try the
following investigation to find out.

Procedure

1. Time the period of a swing as before, but this time
   let the person in the swing pump.
2. Does pumping affect the period of the swing? If so,
   how?

Explanation

When you pump the swing, you are raising the **center
of mass.** This is the point in an object where its mass is
equal in all directions. (For example, objects that spin
rotate around their center of mass.) When you lift your
legs forward and back, your center of mass is higher
than when your legs are straight down. Raising your
center of mass gives you some potential energy (see
"Downhill Racer: The Slide," page 2, for more
information about potential energy), which you convert
into kinetic energy. This makes you swing higher and
higher.

In the "More Fun Stuff to Do" box on the next page,
you can experiment with raising the center of mass of
something that is easier to see and feel: a small pendulum.

Pump It Up

To better understand how pumping works, try this investigation.

1. Make a pendulum by tying a small mass (such as a washer) on the end of a string about 16 inches (.5 m) long. Hold the pendulum in front of you.
2. Start it swinging by pulling the weighted end a few inches to the left or right and then releasing it.
3. When the pendulum reaches the bottom of its swing, lift the pendulum's string up an inch (3 cm) or so. As the pendulum continues its arc and begins to rise, return the pendulum and string to their original height.
4. Continue raising and lowering the pendulum for each swing.
5. What happens to the arc the pendulum is following?

GALILEO'S DAYDREAM
A PENDULUM IS A SWING, TOO!

A pendulum is in fact a falling object, but the string, chain, or rope keeps it from falling straight down. The string puts another force on the pendulum (along with gravity) so that when it swings, it takes a curved path. Galileo studied pendulums when he was a child. As he sat in church, he watched the candelabras swing above his head, suspended by ropes, and started thinking about gravity.

Think about the pendulums that you have seen. What factors do you think influence pendulums? Try a few experiments to learn more.

ACTIVITY 1
HOW LONG DOES IT TAKE?

Procedure

1. Tape a pencil to the top of a desk or table so that half of it sticks out over the edge.
2. Make a pendulum string 10 inches (25 cm) long, with loops tied at each end.
3. Put one loop of your pendulum string on the pencil. Open a paper clip and attach it to the other loop. Put a steel washer on the paper clip. The diagram shows the proper setup.
4. Estimate how many times you think your pendulum will swing in 15 seconds. You should count only complete periods. In a complete period, the washer returns to the place closest to where it was released, going forward and back again for a complete cycle.

5 Hold the washer at a 90° angle—straight out, parallel to the floor, and parallel to the table edge.

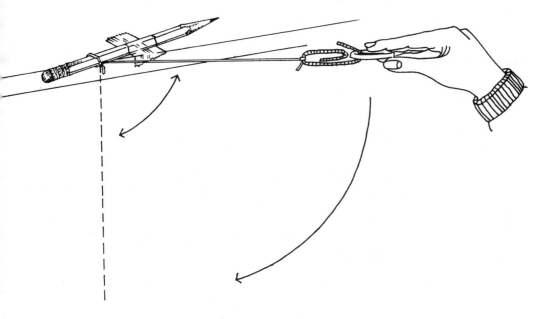

You will probably need a friend to count the 15 seconds for you. At the signal "go," release the pendulum and count the periods until your friend says "stop."

6 Record the number of periods your pendulum made. How close was your estimate?

7 All scientific experiments need to be repeated both by yourself and by others. Repeat the experiment yourself a couple more times, then have a friend do it. Did all the trials give the same results?

Can you think of anything that you can change in the experiment that might affect the outcome of the experiment? Any factor that changes is called a **variable.** With a pendulum, the variables of mass, the angle of swing, and the string length may all have an effect on how long it takes to complete one swing. Try changing these variables and see what happens—but change only one variable at a time, or you won't be able to tell which changed variable caused which changed outcome.

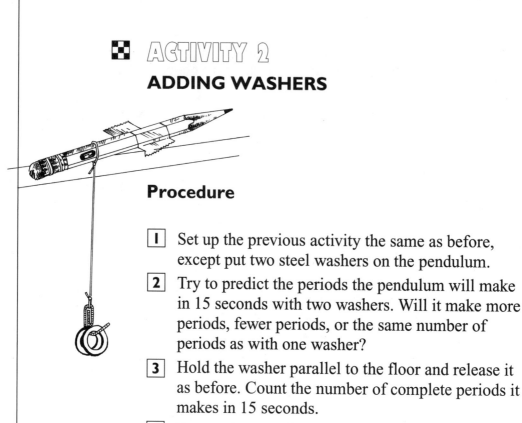

ACTIVITY 2

ADDING WASHERS

Procedure

1. Set up the previous activity the same as before, except put two steel washers on the pendulum.

2. Try to predict the periods the pendulum will make in 15 seconds with two washers. Will it make more periods, fewer periods, or the same number of periods as with one washer?

3. Hold the washer parallel to the floor and release it as before. Count the number of complete periods it makes in 15 seconds.

4. Repeat the experiment several times to see if you always get the same results.

5. Repeat the experiment with three steel washers.

6. Does greater mass, that is, more steel washers, affect the number of periods that a pendulum makes in 15 seconds?

ACTIVITY 3

SWING HIGH, SWING LOW

Procedure

1. Set up the pendulum as in Activity 1 on page 12, with only one steel washer.

2. Instead of releasing the washer from a 90° angle (parallel to the floor), release the washer from about a 45° angle, as shown in the following diagram.

3. Count the number of complete periods made in 15 seconds as before.

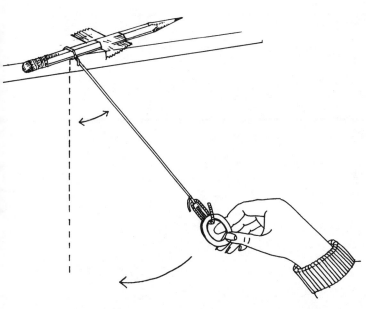

4 Repeat the experiment several times to see if you always get the same results.

5 Does the angle of release affect the period of the pendulum?

■ ACTIVITY 4

LONG ONES, SHORT ONES

Procedure

1 Set up a pendulum the same as in the previous experiment, only this time use a string of a different length.

2 Use the same procedure as the first experiment, releasing the pendulum from a 90° angle.

3 Repeat the experiment several times to see if you always get the same results.

4 Repeat the experiment at least nine more times, using pendulum strings of different length each time. Try some that are longer and some that are shorter. You will use these pendulums in the "More Fun Stuff to Do" section that follows.

5 Does the length of the pendulum string affect the number of periods that a pendulum makes?

Getting the Hang of It

Use the pendulums you just made to find the relationship between the length of the pendulum swing and the number of periods. Use paper clips to make a row of hooks, and number them from 5 to 30. To do this, attach the paper clips to a piece of cardboard that is approximately 3 X 39 inches (8 X 100 cm). Bend one end of each paper clip so it is pointing out and clip one above each number. Tape the paper clips to the cardboard to help hold them in place. The numbers represent the number of periods your pendulums made in 15 seconds.

Hang each pendulum from the hook that corresponds to the number of periods that it made. Look at the pendulums hanging on the hooks. Can you make a general statement about the relationship between the length of the pendulum string and the number of periods that a pendulum makes in 15 seconds? Does the shape of the curve made by the washers look familiar? It's called a parabola, a mathematical shape that is similar to a circle. A **parabola** is the path a thrown object takes due to gravity's pull, as you will see in Chapter 3.

UPSY DAISY
THE SEESAW

The seesaw is an example of a lever. For these experiments you will need at least three friends. Two should weigh about the same, but the others should be of different weights. Weigh everybody before you go to the playground.

ACTIVITY
BALANCING ACT

Procedure

1. Have two friends who weigh about the same sit on opposite sides of the seesaw. The seesaw should be in balance with each person off the ground equally.
2. Have one person lean forward. What happens?
3. Have one person lean backward. What happens?
4. Have two friends who weigh different amounts sit on the ends of the seesaw. Does the seesaw remain balanced?
5. Have the people move in such a way that the seesaw will balance. What did the people have to do to balance?
6. Repeat the experiment using other friends of different weights. Can you see a pattern develop?
7. Put two friends on one side of the seesaw and one on the other. Watch them try to balance the seesaw. What did they have to do to balance?
8. Repeat the experiment, trying different combinations of weights. Can you see a pattern develop?
9. Is it possible for one person to balance three people? How?

Explanation

A seesaw is a simple machine called a **lever**. It has a
lever (a rigid bar used to support a weight—in this case,
the seesaw board) and a **fulcrum** (the support about
which the lever turns—in this case, the pipe the seesaw
moves on).

Two people who weigh about the same can balance
a seesaw if they sit on either end because the force of
gravity is equal on both sides of the fulcrum. They
balance on a point called the center of mass, the place
where the mass of an object—in this case, the lever
and the people—is equal in all directions.

When one person leans forward or backward, he or
she moves the center of mass to a place away from the
fulcrum and out of balance. If the seesaw is out of
balance to begin with, as it was with people of different
weights or with two people on one side, it can be made
to balance if the larger weight is closer than the smaller
weight to the fulcrum. So if the heavier person moves
toward the center of the seesaw, the seesaw will balance.

SPIN YOURSELF SILLY
THE MERRY-GO-ROUND

The merry-go-round is a wonderful place to learn about centripetal force, the force that acts on objects as they move in circles. Try the following investigations while on the playground merry-go-round. You'll need a few friends to help.

ACTIVITY 1
MOVING WATER

Procedure

1. Fill a paper cup half full of water.
2. Sit on the outer edge of the merry-go-round, holding the paper cup, while someone pushes the merry-go-round as fast as possible.
3. What happens to the water? Does it stay level?

■ ACTIVITY 2

MERRY-GO-ROUND CATCH

Get two friends to help you with this activity.

Procedure

1. Sit on the merry-go-round and have one friend sit on the opposite side. The other friend should push the merry-go-round until it spins, and then stand near it and observe.
2. Throw a ball back and forth to the friend who is riding with you.
3. Have both friends describe what they saw. Did they see the same thing?

■ ACTIVITY 3

TAKE AIM

Procedure

1. Sit on the edge of the merry-go-round while it is not spinning.
2. Have a friend stand 10 feet (3 m) away from the merry-go-round.
3. Throw a ball to your friend. Was it easy for your friend to catch it?
4. Next, try to throw the ball to your friend while the merry-go-round is spinning. Was it easy for your friend to catch it? How must you aim in order for your friend to catch it?

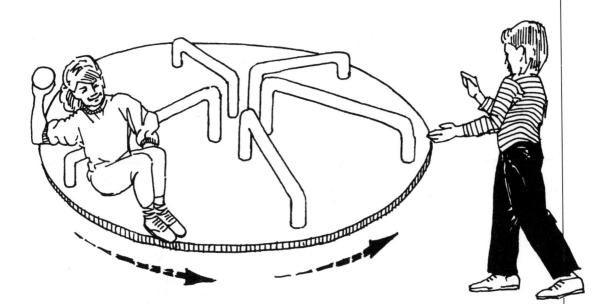

 ACTIVITY 4

SPINNING FASTER

You'll need five or six friends for this last investigation.

Procedure

1. Have everyone sit along the outer edge of the merry-go-round.
2. Get the merry-go-round going fairly fast, then stop pushing.
3. Immediately have everyone move toward the center of the merry-go-round as quickly as possible. Everyone should move at the same time.
4. What happens?

Explanation

Sir Isaac Newton (1642–1727) was the first scientist/mathematician to explain why things move the way they do. **Newton's three laws of motion** explain the forces at work on the merry-go-round. Simply stated, Newton's laws are as follows:

1. An object moving in a straight line will keep moving in that direction unless acted on by an outside force.
2. If an object is moved by a force, it will move in the direction of the force. Also, the greater the force, the faster the object moves.
3. For every action there is an equal and opposite reaction.

These laws are behind the centripetal force created by the spinning merry-go-round. At any moment on the ride, the riders obey Newton's three laws. The riders cannot move in a straight line because they are acted on by an outside force, the merry-go-round itself. Because the merry-go-round is attached to a central pivot point, the ride turns, exerting centripetal force on the riders. The riders feel as though they are being thrown off the ride, especially as the merry-go-round goes faster and centripetal force increases. The water in the paper cup behaves in the same manner. It moves to the outer edge of the cup because of the centripetal force created by the turning ride.

When you throw a ball back and forth on the merry-go-round, the ball goes straight, but your friend continues moving. From your viewpoint on the ride, it looks like the ball curves away from your friend. When you play catch with someone who is not on the ride, you have to aim to one side or the other of that person. The reason is that your turning motion on the ride changes the speed and direction of your throw.

Have you ever watched an ice skater spin in a circle? When the skater brings his or her arms in, the skater spins faster, and when he or she spreads the arms away from the body (and increases the radius of rotation), the skater moves more slowly. The same thing happens with you and your friends on the merry-go-round. When you move toward the center, you give the merry-go-round a smaller radius of rotation, making the ride spin faster.

GRAVITY

MEASURING THE FORCE

A unit that is commonly used to describe forces we feel is the g. One g is equal to the force of earth's gravity. When the space shuttle takes off, the astronauts feel about 3 g's of force (three times the force of earth's gravity). How many g's do you feel on the swings, on your bicycle, on an amusement park ride, or in a car? You can make a g meter to measure these forces.

ACTIVITY

MAKE A G METER

Procedure

1. Trace the g meter in the illustration on the next page.
2. Cut out your tracing of the g meter.
3. Glue your g meter tracing to a 5-by-8-inch (13 × 20-cm) index card or other piece of thin cardboard and trim the card to size.
4. Take about 6 inches (15 cm) of heavy thread and tie one end to a weight such as a washer or key. Tie the other end through the hole at the top of the g meter.
5. Hold the g meter in front of you so that it faces you. Let the thread hang down so that it lines up with the 0 g mark.
6. For the g meter to work properly, the top edge of the meter must be horizontal.
7. When the string moves in either direction of the arrow, the mark it passes over is the force in g's.

HOW TO SET UP YOUR METER

Trace and cut out this g meter.

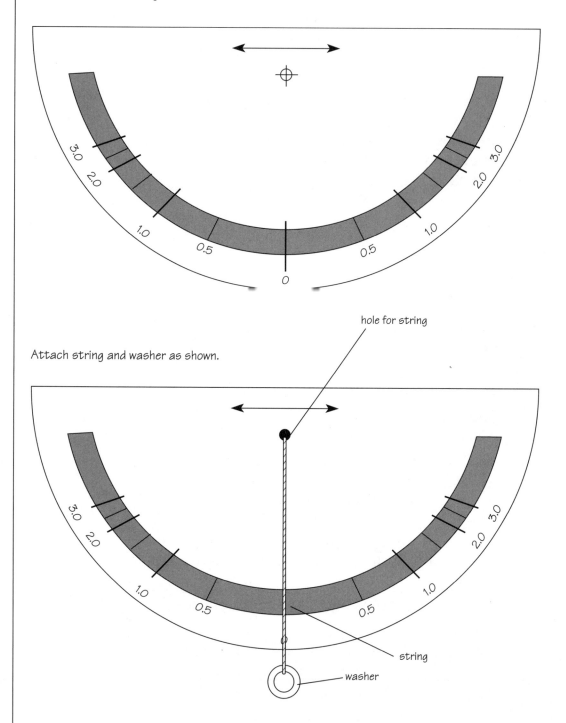

Attach string and washer as shown.

hole for string

string

washer

So That's What I Feel

1. To measure centripetal force when moving in a circle (for example, on the merry-go-round at the playground), hold the g meter so that one end of the arrow points toward the center of the ride. As the ride moves slowly, see how many g's are created. As the ride increases in speed, what happens to the g's?

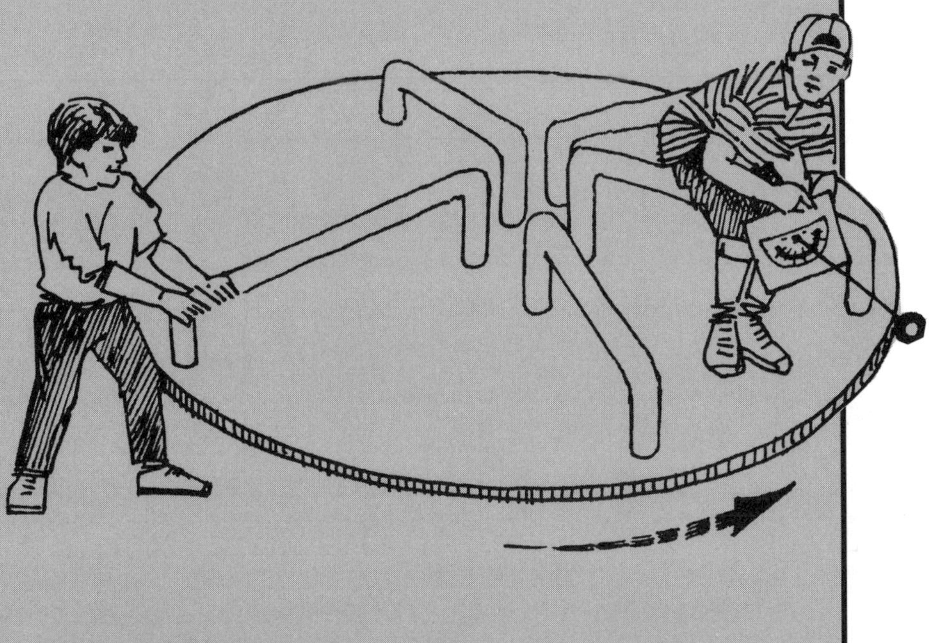

2. To measure g force when starting or stopping (for example, while riding in your parents' car), hold the g meter to your side so that one end of the arrow points in the direction the car is traveling (see the picture on the next page). As the car moves faster and then slower, how many g's do you feel? What happens if the car stops very fast?

(continued)

25

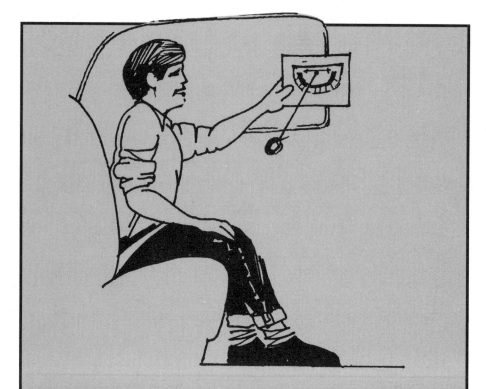

3. Other investigations:

- When your parents drive the car around a corner, hold the g meter in front of you as you did on the merry-go-round. How many g's do you feel? Is there a difference between going around a corner slowly and going around it fast?

- On a swing, hold the g meter beside you so that the arrow points in the direction you are swinging. How many g's do you feel?

- Use the g meter on the merry-go-round at the playground. Sit on the outside edge of the ride and point one end of the arrow toward the center. How many g's does the g meter say you are feeling? What happens to the number of g's as the ride moves faster? What happens to the g's if you sit closer to the center of the ride?

- Use the g meter in the next section on amusement park rides. How many g's does each ride create?

BUBBLES AND TREASURE

BUBBLEOLOGY

Try the following bubble experiment. Maybe you'll be good enough to get your "doctor of bubbleology" degree.

Procedure

1   Begin by making a good bubble-making solution. Half the fun is experimenting and coming up with your own special recipe. In general, mix two parts dishwashing soap (Joy™ works the best) with six parts water. To make stronger bubbles, add one to four parts glycerin. (One part corn syrup will work as well.)

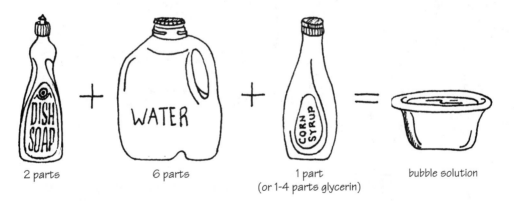

| 2 parts | 6 parts | 1 part (or 1-4 parts glycerin) | bubble solution |

2   Practice your basic bubble-blowing techniques with simple loops made of wire. Experiment with different sizes and shapes of loops to see what types of bubbles you can form.

27

3 Make a bubble frame by running approximately 1.5 feet (0.5 m) of thin string or thread through two straws, then tying it together. Place the frame in the bubble solution, then carefully lift it out so the soap film is stretched across the frame. Can you twist the frame and create interesting shapes? Pull the frame toward you rapidly. Can you create a large bubble? Does a square frame make a square bubble?

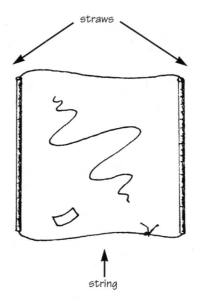

straws

string

4 Wet the surface of a shallow pan with some bubble solution, then wet one end of a straw with bubble solution as well. Hold the end of the straw just above the pan's surface and blow gently until you have created a bubble **hemisphere.** (A hemisphere is half of a sphere; a sphere is any object shaped like a ball.) How big a bubble can you blow?

Try to put several hemispheres in a row to create a
caterpillar bubble. Try to blow one large bubble,
then push the straw farther into it and form
a smaller bubble on the inside.

MORE FUN STUFF TO DO

Bigger, Better Bubbles

Can you design other bubble-blowing devices? Will a straw dipped in the bubble solution work? Will it blow small or big bubbles? Can you make a bubble blower out of a paper cup? Can you blow one bubble inside another bubble in the air?

Explanation

A bubble is held together by **surface tension**, the force of attraction between water molecules that creates a "thin skin" on the surface of the water. Water molecules at the surface are more attracted to each other than to air, that is, they try to stick together. This property enables small insects to walk on the surface of water. However, if the molecules of water stick together too much, bubbles won't form very easily. Soap decreases the surface tension of water to a point that is ideal for making bubbles. The bubbles stick together in a thin layer of soapy water.

However, the water in bubbles tends to evaporate quickly. When the water evaporates, the bubble's wall is broken and the bubble bursts. Usually, a substance such as glycerin or corn syrup is added to the bubble solution to keep the water from evaporating so that the bubbles last longer. Some bubbles can last a long time. Sir Thomas Dewar made a bubble that lasted 108 days, and another physicist, Eiffel Plasterer, blew a bubble that lasted 340 days.

A common question that arises when playing with bubbles is "Why do they always form spheres?" The answer is in the special nature of the sphere. The **sphere** is a ball-like shape that has maximum volume and minimum surface area. Any other shape that has the same volume as the sphere would have a larger surface area.

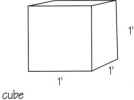

cube
surface area = 6 square feet
volume = 1 cubic foot

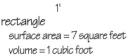

rectangle
surface area = 7 square feet
volume = 1 cubic foot

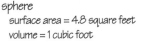

sphere
surface area = 4.8 square feet
volume = 1 cubic foot

The surface of the bubble is **elastic**, which means that the bubble, like a rubber ball, will return to its original shape after being deformed. The sphere is therefore the easiest shape for the bubble to maintain.

❖ ACTIVITY 2

A NATURE TREASURE HUNT—LEAVES AND NEEDLES

While you are at the playground or park, you may want to organize a treasure hunt. The idea is to make a list of many objects that you want to find. A big part of science is finding things in nature and classifying them according to their similar characteristics. There is no limit to the objects that you can put on your list. Who knows what you will find when you go on a treasure hunt for leaves and needles?

Procedure

1. Take along a plastic bag to gather your collection and paper and pencils to make pictures of your discoveries. Look for as many different kinds of leaves and needles as you can.

2. Hunt by yourself or with a group of friends. If lots of people go on the hunt, form groups and see which group can find the most. Give everyone lots of time.

3. When the hunt is over, take a good look at your collections. How many different kinds of needles did you find? How many different kinds of leaves? If you hunted in groups, compare collections. Which group found the most? Who found the most unusual leaf or needle?

4. Now use a piece of paper and a pencil to draw or trace the different leaf shapes. Can you put the leaves into groups that have common characteristics? For example, needles and leaves are themselves two groups. The classification of living things into groups with common characteristics is an important skill that every scientist needs.

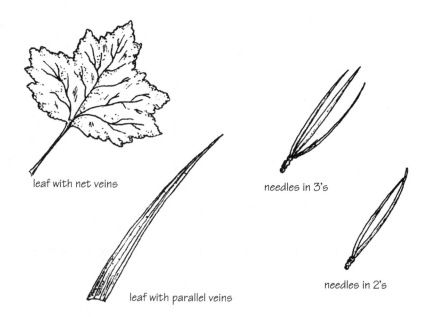

leaf with net veins

needles in 3's

leaf with parallel veins

needles in 2's

Found Objects

This treasure hunt is best done with two or three evenly matched teams. It is a race against the clock and against each other. Provide each team with a list of objects, paper, a pencil, and a plastic bag. Make sure someone on the team has a watch. Before sending the teams off on their search through the park or playground, set a time limit. Forty-five minutes should be enough.

As each team finds an item, have one team member cross it off the list and put the object in the plastic bag. The team that collects the most objects within the time limit—or completes the list first—wins.

Remind all players to stay with their teams and not to trespass on private property.

Here are some things that you might want to add to your list:

- Three kinds of leaves
- Three kinds of needles
- A feather
- A seed
- A nut or an acorn
- A pinecone
- A clover leaf (or a four-leaf clover)
- A pure white rock
- Two kinds of flowers
- A piece of tree bark
- Some litter (such as an aluminum can)

Round and Round We Go
Amusement Park Rides

Amusement parks are one of the best places
to go for fun, but they're also practical places that
show physics and engineering in action. Next time
you visit an amusement park, try to see the
science that is all around you.

WHERE IT ALL BEGAN

A BRIEF HISTORY OF AMUSEMENT PARKS

Most of us enjoy the time we spend in amusement parks, but some people get a little carried away. A computer operator with the Internal Revenue Service has ridden the Beast, a wooden roller coaster at the Kings Island Amusement Park outside Cincinnati, over 4,357 times and spent an estimated three months waiting in line!

What is it that draws us to amusement parks with their monster roller coasters? A new steel coaster at Cedar Point Amusement Park in Sandusky, Ohio, has a 60° first drop from a height of a 20-story building. It's been said it is like riding in a car with your head out the window at 70 miles per hour (110 kmph)—but to get the full effect, you'd have to drive it off a cliff. This is fun?

On the Shock Wave, a looped coaster at the Six Flags Great America Amusement Park in Gurnee, Illinois, riders are lifted 17 stories, dropped heftily at 70 miles per hour (110 kmph), sent into a giant loop that turns them upside down, then thrown into a "boomerang" that rapidly reverses direction in a pretzel-like turn and sends them finally through a series of corkscrew spirals.

Both of these amusements are the most popular rides at their parks. The lines of people waiting to ride them never lets up. We pay money, good money, to be scared to death.

Current amusement park rides originated in several places. The roller coaster began in 15th-century Russia as an ice slide. Built in St. Petersburg, this early slide was made from a wooden frame 70 feet (21 m) high that was packed with snow and watered down. Riders rode down these hills on blocks of ice that were slightly hollowed out to fit their bodies.

From these early beginnings, other gravity-powered rides, known as Russian Mountains, evolved in Europe and later in the United States. The first roller coaster in North America was built by LaMarcus Thompson at Coney Island in 1884. His Scenic Railway was an immediate hit with its top speed of 6 miles per hour (10 kmph). Coasters became more popular as they increased in both size and speed. In the 1920s there were over 1,500 roller coasters in North America. The depression and World War II led to the coaster's decline to the point where there are only about 150 today.

Of equal importance was the creation of the Ferris wheel, originally built for the 1893 Chicago Columbian Exposition. It was designed by George Washington Ferris and was modeled after the structural principles of the bicycle wheel. Ferris first got the idea for his ride when he was in elementary school, but building one took him many years.

The first Ferris wheel was nearly 300 feet (91 m) tall and 30 feet (9 m) wide. It had 36 pendulum cars, each able to hold 60 passengers. The axle of the incredible structure was a manufacturing feat without parallel—the largest single piece of steel ever forged to date. Like the roller coaster before it, the Ferris wheel enjoyed tremendous popularity and smaller copies of the original soon sprang up everywhere.

Few things have managed to survive the changing times and tastes as well as amusement parks have. Although they declined in popularity in the 1930s and 1940s, they were reborn in the 1950s in the theme park, the brainchild of Walt Disney. The notion of organizing amusement parks around a theme offered a completely new gimmick for the amusement industry. Disneyland the theme park and the Disney television shows ("The Wonderful World of Disney" and also "The Mickey Mouse Club") took off in popularity, and amusement parks have never been the same since.

THE KING OF THE RIDES
THE ROLLER COASTER

Roller coasters were originally made of wood and rode on steel wheels. Later versions followed paths of steel and rolled on air-filled tires. But they all work on basically the same principle: gravity. The park charges to take you to the top of the first hill, and gravity gives you the rest of the ride for free. Of course, the park also ensures that you get safely back to the starting point.

ACTIVITY
FEEL THE FORCES

Procedure

As you ride the roller coaster, try to experience the ride as you would conduct any other science experiment. You are the experiment. Note when you feel increased and decreased forces. They may push you into your seat or lift you off it. They may push you to the left or right. As you ride, try to answer the following questions:

1. How does the size of the hills change during the ride?
2. Do you move faster or slower when you are at the top of a hill?
3. Do you move faster or slower when you are at the bottom of a hill?
4. As you go up a hill, do you gain or lose speed?
5. As you go down a hill, do you gain or lose speed?
6. As you go up a hill, do you feel heavier, lighter, or your usual weight?
7. As you go down a hill, do you feel heavier, lighter, or your usual weight?

Making the Next Great American Scream Machine

You can create your own roller coaster in your backyard. All you need is a garden hose, some marbles, and a few bricks or blocks of wood. Use two hoses laid side by side, or fold one garden hose back on itself in such a way that it creates two parallel tubes.

Start your "roller coaster" design by putting one end higher on a picnic table or a chair. From there you can create hills and valleys using lawn chairs, bricks, blocks of wood, or anything else you can think of. The marbles will be the roller coaster cars. Place them at the start of the ride and let gravity do the rest. Experiment with your design and make changes as necessary. Maybe you will even come up with a new idea for a roller coaster.

marble

hoses

8   When the ride makes a turn, are you pushed into the turn or away from it?

9   When the tracks curve, do they tilt inward or outward or are they parallel to the ground?

Explanation

A roller coaster works because of two things: gravity and the law of conservation of energy (explained in "Downhill Racer: The Slide," page 2). A roller coaster is similar to a slide except it is longer and you ride in a train car rather than on the seat of your pants. The wheels reduce friction: it's easier to let something roll than to let it slide.

The diagram shows a section of a roller coaster.

maximum potential energy

Each hill must be lower than the one before because friction causes loss of energy.

Motor carries you to the top of the hill.

maximum kinetic energy

Unlike riding a slide, you don't have to climb to the top of the first hill on the roller coaster. A motor does the work. But as on the slide, you start with potential energy. That potential energy is turned into kinetic energy as gravity pulls you down the first hill. The farther you go down the hill, the more potential energy is changed into kinetic energy, which you feel as speed. The ride goes fastest at the bottom of the hill because all the potential energy has been changed to kinetic energy.

As you go up the next hill, kinetic energy is changed back into potential energy and the ride slows down. The higher you go, the more energy is changed and you feel the car slow down. This conversion of kinetic energy to potential energy and vice versa continues as you go up and down hills for the rest of the ride. The total energy does not increase or decrease; it just changes from one form to the other.

However, some of the energy is changed into friction. Wind resistance, the rolling of the wheels, and other factors all use some of the energy. Coaster designers know that friction plays a part in the ride. Therefore, they make each successive hill lower so that the coaster will be able to make it over each peak.

The force that you feel when the coaster makes a turn is called centripetal force (explained in "Downhill Racer: The Slide," page 2). When you make a turn, it feels as though you are being thrown to the outside of the car. Coaster designers take this into account when they bank the turns by tilting the track. Centripetal force then pushes you against your seat so that you aren't thrown out of the car.

LOOP THE LOOP
THE LOOPING COASTER

Much of the excitement around roller coaster rides centers on the ones that loop or go through a corkscrew. You experience not only the thrills of tremendous speed and falling from great heights, but also the exhilaration of being turned upside down in the process.

ACTIVITY
THE TURNING OF THE CORKSCREW

Procedure

As you ride the looping or corkscrew roller coaster, see if you can answer the following questions.

1. If the ride has corkscrews, do the circles get wider or narrower, or do they stay the same?
2. When you are turned upside down in a corkscrew, are you pushed down in your seat or are you lifted off the seat?
3. When you enter a loop, do you feel heavier or lighter than you normally do?
4. When you reach the top of a loop, do you feel heavier or lighter than you normally do?
5. Do you feel a greater force when you enter a loop or when you leave it?
6. When you go up in a loop, does the train speed up or slow down?
7. How does the force you feel in your neck when you go forward through a loop compare to what you feel when you go backward?

Explanation

If you look at the shape of the curve in a looping roller coaster, you will see that it is not a circle but a teardrop shape. That shape is called a **clothoid loop**. It was first described by mathematical genius Leonard Euler of Switzerland in the 18th century. Only recently did roller coaster engineers realize that it was the perfect shape for achieving the long sought after goal of the roller coaster somersault.

clothoid loop

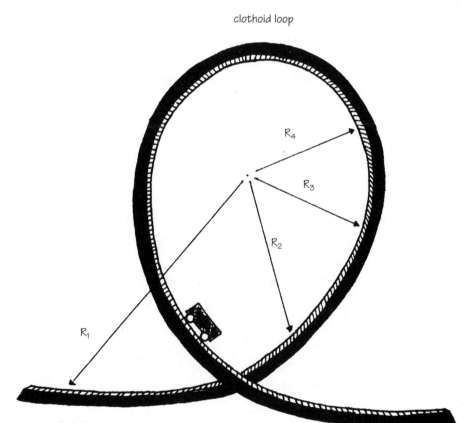

R_4

R_3

R_2

R_1

A clothoid is a circle whose radius gets progressively smaller: $R_1 > R_2 > R_3 > R_4$.

Before using Euler's ideas, designers had little success with what seemed to be the logical choice for the loop, a 360° circle. Simple physics doomed that shape. All rides moving in a vertical circle generate centripetal force that presses the riders into their seats. At the top of a loop, when the coaster and its occupants are upside down, the centripetal force must be greater than the force of gravity or the people will fall out of their seats.

Designers can make the ride fast enough and the circle big enough to create just over 1 g of centripetal force to counteract gravity (1 g) at the top of the circle. Unfortunately, in order to achieve 1 g of force at the top of the circle, riders would have to be subjected to over 8 g's when they first enter the loop.

Eight g's are a lot for the human body to handle. To put it in perspective, the space shuttle creates only about 3 g's. At 6 g's many people get nosebleeds, and at 9 g's unconsciousness can occur.

The clothoid loop smooths out the forces that the riders undergo and still keeps them safe. It does this by being a circle whose radius continually decreases on the upward swing. This decrease in radius creates a higher centripetal force at a slower speed and allows riders to undergo a maximum of 3 to 4 g's on entering the loop.

This innovation allows vertical loops to be quite large. The Shock Wave, a looping coaster at Six Flags in Gurnee, Illinois, has a 130-foot (40-m) loop 13 stories above the ground that sends riders head over heels. The loop is safe because of physics, mathematics, and engineering.

PUT A NEW SPIN ON IT

THE CAROUSEL AND OTHER CENTRIPETAL FORCE RIDES

The law of conservation of energy governs and helps explain the operation of many of the rides at amusement parks. Another important set of laws are Newton's three laws of motion. These laws are especially important on the centripetal force rides, such as the merry-go-round and others that go in a circle. Centripetal force causes you to feel as though you are being thrown to the side of a ride as it moves in a circle.

As you try the centripetal force rides, try to experience the ride as if it were a science experiment. Feel the forces acting on your body and note where you are on the ride when the forces occur.

ACTIVITY 1

THE CAROUSEL

When you take this ride, think about the following questions.

Procedure

1. As the ride turns, is your body thrown slightly to the inside or the outside?

2. Do all the ride animals go up and down at the same time?

3. Does the ride animal next to you move up and down as you do?

4. Do you feel slightly lighter or slightly heavier when your horse is going up? What about when it's going down?

5. Which ride animals move faster around the circle—the ones on the inside or the ones on the outside?

✦ MORE FUN STUFF TO DO ✦

1. An important part of carousel design is the artwork of the animals. Look at the artwork. Which is your favorite?

2. Can you design a ride animal that could be used on the ride?

3. Ask someone at the park when the merry-go-round was built. Did it have a history before it came to the park?

▨ ACTIVITY 2

THE SCRAMBLER

The Scrambler is a more complex centripetal force ride in which there are two axes of rotation.

Procedure

1. Before you get on the ride, can you figure out the path that the seats follow during the ride? What effect does the double rotation have on the path?

2. As you ride, are you moving faster when you are closer to or farther from the ride's center?

3. Are you pushed inward or outward as the ride makes the turns?

4. Are the forces on the ride always the same?

5. Are there times when you feel as though the ride is moving in a straight line?

46

♦ MORE FUN STUFF TO DO ♦

Which Way Did I Go?

What is the path that you actually take on a ride like the Scrambler that has two axes of rotation? To find out, get a Spirograph™ from a toy store. Use two circles with approximately the same proportions as the amusement ride, that is, the inner circle should be less than half the size of the outer circle. What pattern do these two circles make?

■ ACTIVITY 3

SWINGING CHAIRS

If your amusement park has a swinging chair ride, ride it and try to answer the following questions.

Procedure

1. Which goes higher—an empty swing or one with someone in it?
2. What do you feel as the speed increases?
3. What happens to the seats as the speed increases?

Explanation

As mentioned in Chapter 1, Newton's three laws of motion play an important part in the operation of the rides at an amusement park. These laws are the physics behind the centripetal force rides. For example, on a ride sometimes called the Music Machine (a high-speed centripetal force ride), the riders move around in a circle. The ride provides a good illustration of Newton's three laws of motion. The riders try to move in a straight line (Newton's first law). However, they are acted on by an outside force (centripetal force). Because the ride seat is attached to a central pivot point, the ride seat moves in a circle and exerts centripetal force in that direction (Newton's second law). At the same time, the riders exert an equal and opposite force on the ride seat (Newton's third law). They feel as though they are being thrown outward in the seat when they are actually obeying Newton's three laws of motion. The riders try to move in a straight line, but because the ride seat curves, centripetal force makes the riders move along the lines created by that force. The riders sense this as being thrown outward on the ride.

Several physicists have tried to figure out the exact path riders take on the Scrambler. The most common method used to determine the path was to program a computer to draw the path. The computer usually drew the path shown in the first diagram at the left.

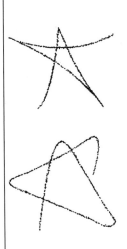

Last summer I decided to conduct my own simple experiment by actually riding the Scrambler, rather than using a computer. I rode with a large squirt gun and traced a trail of water right below my seat. You know what? The computer was wrong. I traced two different paths, depending on which seat I rode in, as shown in the second and third diagrams at the left. Sometimes conducting a science experiment the old-fashioned way is better than using a computer!

As for the swinging chairs, both an empty seat and one with a person in it will reach the same height. That's because both gravity (pulling the rider down) and centripetal force (making the rider go in a circle) depend on the mass of an object. An empty chair has less of both forces acting on it, and it rises to the same height as a chair with a person in it.

LOOK WHAT'S TURNING UP
VERTICAL CIRCLES

Fun things start to happen when circular rides are turned
on end so that they move like a wheel. The centripetal
force that the ride creates combines with the force
of gravity, and the results can be as exciting as a ride
on the space shuttle.

ACTIVITY 1
FERRIS WHEEL

Procedure

Ride the Ferris wheel and try to answer the following questions.

1. When the Ferris wheel is going full speed, do you feel lighter or heavier at the bottom of the circle? How does this compare to the way you feel at the top of the circle?
2. Do the forces get stronger or weaker as the speed increases?

✦ ACTIVITY 2

ROTATING PLATFORM

If your amusement park has a rotating platform, ride it and try to answer the following questions.

Procedure

1. When the ride is going full speed, do you feel lighter or heavier at the bottom of the circle? How does this compare to the way you feel at the top of the circle?
2. What happens to you when the ride is halfway down? Halfway up?
3. What happens to you at the top of the circle?
4. Does it make a difference if you sit on the left side or right side of the ride?

Explanation

The forces that you feel are the combination of the centripetal force the ride creates (because it's moving in a circle) and the force of gravity. At the bottom of the circle, the forces amplify each other so you feel heavier. At the top of the circle, they cancel each other out and you feel lighter.

It is common on some vertical circle rides, like the rotating platforms, for the centripetal force to be equal to earth's gravity. This means that at the bottom of the circle you feel 2 g's (twice earth's gravity) and at the top of the circle you feel weightless.

These values are similar to what you'd feel on a ride on the space shuttle. At launch, you would feel between 2 and 3 g's. Once in orbit, you would feel weightless due to the microgravity in space. **Microgravity** is a gravitational force that is less than the force of gravity at the surface of the earth. Astronauts experience microgravity when they are in orbit around the earth.

CRASH, CRASH, CRASH
BUMPER CARS

The bumper cars are a fun place to learn how not to drive. But at least your car insurance doesn't cost more after the experience. Some people try to avoid being hit, while others want to be crashed into. Some drive around sedately, while others run into everything in the driving area.

ACTIVITY
IMPULSIVE DRIVING

Procedure

It is the crashes that we are most interested in for the following experiments. Try to answer the following questions.

1. Before you get on the ride, look at the bumper cars. How are they different from a normal car?
2. When you first start up your car, which way are you pushed?
3. When your car stops, which way are you thrown?
4. If you are in a head-on crash, which way are you thrown?
5. When you are hit from behind by another car, which way are you thrown?
6. What happens to you when you are hit from the side?
7. When your car is moving and it runs into someone else's car, when do you feel the greatest force— when the other car isn't moving, when it is moving away from you, or when it is moving toward you?

Explanation

The bumper cars obey Newton's three laws of motion. According to the first law, objects (like people in bumper cars) tend to keep traveling in the direction that they are going. This means that when your car is moving and it hits someone else's car and that person's car stops, your body obeys Newton's first law and keeps going forward. Similarly, when your car is stopped and someone else hits it from behind and moves it forward, you try to keep your body stopped and you feel as though you are being thrown backward (as though you are getting a minor whiplash).

The second principle of science in bumper cars is that of **impulse** and **momentum**. Impulse and momentum are what Newton called "the quantity of motion." Impulse is the product of a force and the time interval over which it acts. This impulse is transferred to an object, giving it momentum. Momentum is the product of the mass and the **velocity** of an object. Velocity is speed in a specific direction.

When your car crashes into another car that is stopped, some of the momentum is transferred to the other car from yours, making the other car move. Some of your momentum is converted into an impulse that causes the other bumper car to move. It will have momentum equal to the impulse it received. The rubber bumpers that surround the cars slow down the transfer of momentum, making it less likely that anyone will get hurt.

MADE YOU LOOK
FUN HOUSE MIRRORS

When you look at yourself in your bathroom mirror, what do you see? It's an exact image of you, only switched from left to right. You may have seen other kinds of mirrors as well. Convex (curved out) and concave (curved in) mirrors will also reflect your image, only you may appear to be upside down, smaller, or larger. But it is in the fun house mirror that really strange things begin to happen.

ACTIVITY
STRANGE LOOKS

Procedure

If you have a fun house mirror at your amusement park, try the following activities. If you want, you can construct a fun house mirror of your own by carefully bending a sheet of shiny metal into the S-shaped curve that you find in a fun house mirror.

1. Are you right-side-up or upside down in the mirror?
2. Move up and down in front of the mirror. Does your image change? How?
3. Part of the mirror curves toward you and part curves away. How is the image different in each section? Or is the image the same?
4. Move your right hand up and down. Is the image in the mirror upside down?
5. Is everything in the mirror in focus?

Explanation

Light bounces off an object and heads toward the mirror. If you look in a regular, flat mirror, like the one in your bathroom, the light bounces off it at the same angle. (That's one simple law of reflecting light: it reflects at the same angle it went in.) When the reflected light hits the lens of your eye, it is focused at one point on your retina, creating a **point retinal image**. The image is in focus.

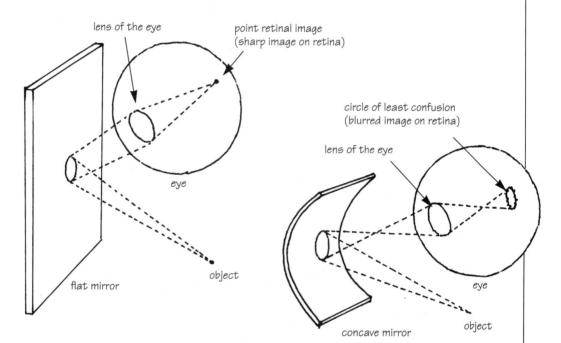

In a concave mirror, the light gets bounced off in unusual directions. The lens of your eye tries to focus the light bouncing off the mirror, but it can't quite do it.

Rather than focus all the light, and therefore the image, at one point, the concave mirror causes the image to spread out and be blurred. The area where the blurred image hits the retina is called the **circle of least confusion.** The brain tries to interpret that image as best it can and creates a distorted, confused image. It's easier to understand how a flat mirror works, but it's more fun to play with a fun house mirror.

SPLISH, SPLASH
WATER PARKS

Have you ever been to a water park? It's a special kind of amusement park—and the most fun on a really hot day. You can learn science and beat the heat at the same time!

ACTIVITY
THE SLIPPERY SLIDE

Procedure

Go down several different water slides and try to answer the following questions:

1. What is the purpose of the water?
2. What happens when you go down higher slides?
3. In the turns, are you pushed to the inside or the outside of the slide?
4. What happens as you go farther down the slide?
5. Do you go down the slide faster sitting up or lying down?
6. What happens when you reach the pool at the bottom of the slide?
7. Do you go farther in the pool when you ride a mat?
8. What can you do to go farther in the pool at the bottom of the slide?
9. Do lighter or heavier people go farther in the pool when they reach the bottom of the slide?

Explanation

The water slide at a water park is similar to both the slide and the roller coaster. As with the slide, the higher the hill, the faster you go when you reach the bottom. As with the roller coaster, you go down the hill faster and faster because of the acceleration caused by gravity. The water helps to reduce friction. If the slide has a turn, you feel as though you are being thrown to the outside edge. By now you should know why (see the explanation of "The Curved Slide," page 3, if you need a reminder).

When you reach the pool at the bottom of the slide, you skip on the surface of the water. You stay on the surface because the surface tension of the water is greater than the downward force of gravity. However, friction between you and the water causes you to slow down and you begin to sink. Lighter people, or those who ride a mat, tend to stay on the surface longer.

3

Play Ball!
Sports and Recreational Activities

Have you ever wondered why the flight of a baseball curves, why a paper airplane flies so well (sometimes), or how you can sail a sailboat into the wind? Have you ever been curious about how a particular toy works or if it would work the same way on the moon? These and other questions will soon be answered.

BATTER UP

BERNOULLI'S PRINCIPLE AND THE CURVEBALL

A solid has a definite shape, but liquids and gases assume the shape of the container that holds them. Both liquids and gases are considered fluids; that is, they will flow and offer little resistance when their shape is changed. It is in the motion of these fluids that interesting things can happen.

ACTIVITY 1

GOING UP

Procedure

To see the effect of a moving fluid (in this case, a gas—air), try this experiment.

1. Take an $8^1/_2 \times 11$-inch (2×28-cm) sheet of paper.
2. Place one short end of paper against your chin.
3. Blow hard across the top surface. What happens?

movement
of air

Explanation

The strip rises when you blow on the top of the paper. This provides a perfect illustration of **Bernoulli's principle**, named for the Swiss scientist Daniel Bernoulli, which states that when any fluid, such as air, flows, its pressure decreases when its speed increases. The air above the paper moves faster than the air below it. This creates a lower air pressure above the paper, and the higher pressure below the paper makes the paper rise.

 ## ACTIVITY 2
THE FLOATING CARD

Procedure

This experiment also demonstrates Bernoulli's principle.

1. On a 3 × 5–inch (7.6 × 12.7–cm) card, draw diagonal lines to join opposite corners. The lines intersect in the center of the card.
2. Push a thumbtack through the center of the card.

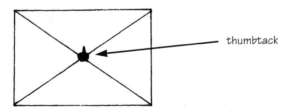

thumbtack

3. Hold the card under a thread spool so that the thumbtack is in the spool hole.

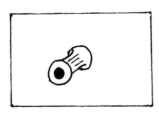

4 Hold and lift the card and the spool and blow hard down the hole with a long, continous breath.

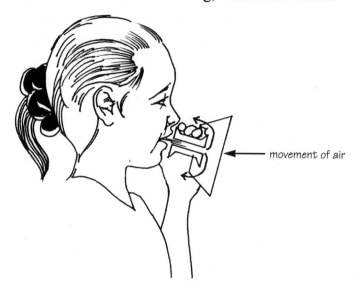

movement of air

5 Take your hand away from the card while blowing. Can you blow the card off the spool?

Explanation

The stream of air that you blow down the spool hole passes between the spool and the card. Because this air moves fast, it creates a lower pressure than that on the opposite side of the card and pushes the card up onto the spool. The harder you blow, the more pressure you create.

⬛ ACTIVITY 3

THE CURVEBALL

So what does Bernoulli's principle have to do with throwing a curveball? Plenty! When a pitcher throws a ball with a lot of spin, part of the spin is in the direction of the air flow and part of the spin is in the opposite direction of the air flow. On the side where the spin and the air flow move in the same direction, there is an increase in air speed.

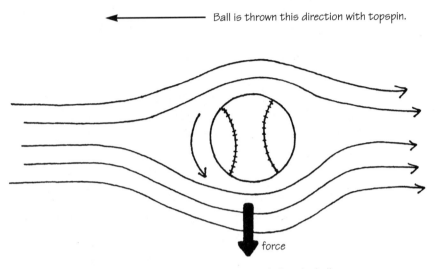

Ball is thrown this direction with topspin.

force

The rotation of the ball makes more air move below the ball—it moves faster and creates lower pressure, a downward force, and the ball drops more than normal.

As shown in the two previous activities, an increase in air speed creates a small decrease in air pressure. This makes the ball, pushed by the higher pressure above it, move in the direction of the lower pressure. As the ball continues to spin on its flight to the plate, it curves from the normal flight of a ball that is thrown without a lot of spin.

Procedure

Get a Wiffle plastic ball or a Ping-Pong ball and try to throw a curveball yourself.

1 First, throw the ball normally to a friend. Does it curve? It should! Gravity will naturally pull it down.

2 Next, try to throw the ball so that it has topspin on it. Does it curve more than normal?

3 Now try to throw the ball with sidespin. Can you get it to curve to the left or the right?

4 What can you do to make it curve more?

5 Can you make it curve upward?

HITTING A MAJOR LEAGUE PITCHER

Do slight changes in the ball's position (a curveball) or changes in speed (a fastball) really have that much effect on a batter's ability to hit the ball? Consider the science behind hitting a ball.

A good pitcher in the major leagues can throw a ball at a speed of between 90 and 100 miles per hour (144 and 160 kmph). What does that mean to a batter? The chart shows how long it will take a ball thrown by a pitcher to reach the plate, according to the speed at which it is thrown.

Speed of Pitch				Time for Ball to Reach the Plate (in seconds)
mph	kmph	ft per sec	mps	
50	80	73	28	0.83
70	112	103	38	0.59
90	144	132	48	0.46
100	160	146	53	0.41

These speeds don't give a batter much time to decide what to do. If you figure that it takes about 0.3 second to actually swing, the batter may have only 0.1 to 0.2 second to decide *where* to swing. The ball will be over the plate for only about 0.01 second, and the bat not only has to be there on time, but also has to be in the right place to hit the ball. It's truly amazing that the human body can perform at this speed.

OTHER THROWN BALLS
IT'S MATHEMATICAL

ACTIVITY 1
THE SHAPE OF YOUR THROW

This experiment is best done outside with a tennis ball.

Procedure

1. Have two friends stand about 5 yards (5 m) apart and facing each other. Stand midway between them, about 10 yards (10 m) to the side, so that you are in a position to observe the flight of the ball.

2. Have your friends play a game of catch, throwing the ball between themselves. They should make several throws of each of the following types.

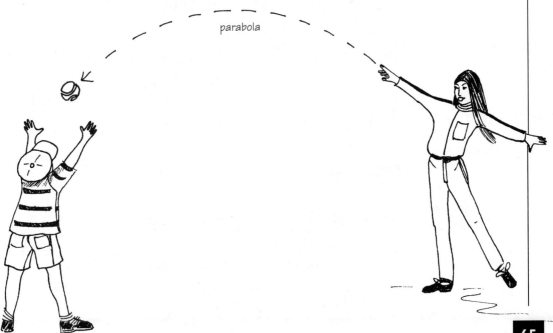

parabola

3. The first throw should be straight across.

4. The second throw should be low, as if your friends were throwing the ball over a fence.

5. The third throw should be higher, as if they were throwing it over a house.

6. The last throw should be even higher, as if they were throwing it over the school gymnasium.

7. What is the shape of the path of a thrown ball?

Explanation

The curved path that the ball takes is called a parabola. It looks like a section of a circle in which the ends have been straightened out. This distinctive curved shape is caused by gravity's effect on a thrown object. The parabola is very important in many areas of science and mathematics.

ACTIVITY 2

HOW HIGH CAN THE BALL GO?

You will need a friend to help you with this experiment. You will also need a stopwatch. (Many digital watches have this capability.) Have your friend be the timer and you be the thrower. Later you can trade places.

Procedure

1. Throw the ball as high as you can. Try to throw the ball straight up.

2. The timer should start the stopwatch the instant the ball leaves your hand. Stop the timing the instant the ball hits the ground.

3 Repeat the experiment several times, then calculate the average time the ball is up by adding the times together, then dividing by the number of throws.

4 Since the average time represents the time the ball is going up plus the time the ball is coming down, divide the average time by 2 to get just the time up.

5 Next, square the time up (multiply it by itself).

6 If you are using feet, multiply the result by 14 to get the height of your throw in feet.

7 If you are using meters, multiply the result by 4.9 to get the height of your throw in meters.

8 How high can you throw a ball?

Formula:

(time up $\times$ time up) $\times$ 14 = the height you can throw a ball, in feet

or

(time up $\times$ time up) $\times$ 4.9 = the height you can throw a ball, in meters

THE FABULOUS FLYING DISK
THE FRISBEE™

In the 1950s, Fred Morrison, a California building inspector and part-time inventor, developed the Pluto Platter, the forerunner of the Frisbee. Although the disks appeared to fly, he told prospective customers that the disks actually rode an invisible wire. He demonstrated the miracle disk at county fairs and sidewalk sales, offering the invisible wire for a penny a foot and throwing in a free disk with every 100-foot purchase.

The Wham-O Toy Company bought Morrison's invention in 1957, altered the design a few years later, and renamed it Frisbee, after the Frisbee Pie Company of Bridgeport, Connecticut. Legend has it that Frisbee pie tins were the original flying disks, used by students at nearby Yale University in the days before plastic.

When two students from the Massachusetts Institute of Technology began a study of the Frisbee in 1965, they asked Wham-O about the engineering that went into the development of the Frisbee. They were told, "There isn't any. But if you can figure out why the thing flies, let us know."

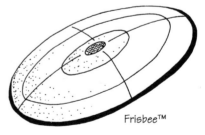
Frisbee™

ACTIVITY

THE FLIGHT OF THE FRISBEE

Procedure

A Frisbee can be a lot of fun to play with, even if you don't know how it works. Take a Frisbee and a friend to the park for this experiment.

1. Can it be thrown better with a backhand flick or a forehand toss?

2. Hold it perfectly flat and throw it. Then tilt the front side up slightly and throw it. Which gives the better flight?

3. Increase the angle of your throw. Can you make the Frisbee come back to you?

4. Does the amount of spin have an effect on the flight of the Frisbee?

5. How must you throw a Frisbee to make it curve to the left or the right?

6. Try throwing it upside down and see what happens.

Explanation

There is a real lack of research into why the Frisbee flies, although some scientists are willing to hazard a guess (other than the invisible wire theory). "The best way to describe it is as a combination airplane wing and gyroscope," says Michael Gold in "The Fairy Tale Physics of Frisbees" (see *Newton at the Bat: The Science in Sports* in the Bibliography). "If you try to say any more than that, it gets real complicated."

What keeps a Frisbee aloft is probably its platelike shape and its ability to fly forward with its front end tipped up at a slight "angle of attack." Any disk thrown at this angle will deflect air toward the ground, exerting an equal and opposite force on the disk that causes it to rise. Bernoulli's principle probably comes into play as well. As the air moving over the top of the Frisbee increases in speed, the pressure decreases, causing the Frisbee to rise.

In addition, the spin creates a gyroscopic effect. A rotating object, whether a football, baseball, or bicycle wheel, has a strong tendency to maintain its orientation in space. The faster it spins, the more it holds its position. Thus, the spinning Frisbee tends to maintain a stable flight.

GO FOR A RIDE
THE BICYCLE

The first bicycles were not pedaled but were pushed along by the feet. This made going downhill easy, but going uphill was difficult. Bicycles were novelties rather than a serious means of transportation until Kirkpatrick Macmillan, a blacksmith, invented the pedal-operated bicycle in Britain in 1839. Improvements in design have continued ever since. The bicycle remains a major form of transportation in many countries.

Go out for a ride on your bicycle. Get a feel for how it rides. What makes it seem so easy to ride? The bicycle is very stable when you ride it, but the reasons are not so clear-cut. In fact, scientists have yet to come up with a simple explanation for the bicycle's stability. What is the science behind it?

ACTIVITY 1
STAYING UP

Procedure

Try the following experiment with a gyroscope.

1. Try to balance the gyroscope on its end. What happens?
2. Next, spin the gyroscope and observe it. What happens? What does the spin do to the gyroscope?
3. What happens as the gyroscope begins to spin slower?

Explanation

The gyroscope follows a variation on Newton's first law of motion. (See the explanation in "Spin Yourself Silly: The Merry-Go-Round," page 19.) In the case of the gyroscope, the motion of the gyroscope (its spinning) keeps it moving in relatively the same position without falling over. The rotational axis will stay oriented in the same direction.

How does the way a gyroscope keeps spinning explain why a bicycle is stable when you ride it? Well, a bicycle is similar to a gyroscope. If the bicycle isn't moving and you try to stand it up, it will fall over fairly easily. However, a moving bicycle can be kept upright fairly easily. Even a moving bicycle without a rider, if given a good push, will roll for a short distance before it falls over. This means that the rolling wheels must act as gyroscopes, helping to keep the bicycle in an upright position.

But there has to be more to it than that. One scientist put extra wheels on a bicycle that would spin in opposite directions to the ones used in riding and thus counteract the gyroscopic action. Although the bicycle was indeed less stable, it could still be ridden.

Another thing that makes the bicycle stable is trail, the distance between the point of contact where the front tire touches the ground and the imaginary point where the front fork, if extended, would touch the ground. (The front fork is the section of the frame that attaches the front wheel to the bicycle and that is connected to the handlebars, allowing the rider to steer the bicycle.) The larger the trail, the more stable the bicycle. A bicycle with a smaller trail will be less stable but more maneuverable.

Look at the trails of different types of bicycles—BMX bikes, mountain bikes, touring bicycles, and so on. Which bicycles have a large trail and which ones have a small trail? Children's bicycles and motorcycles are usually designed to have a relatively large trail, since these bikes need to be more stable.

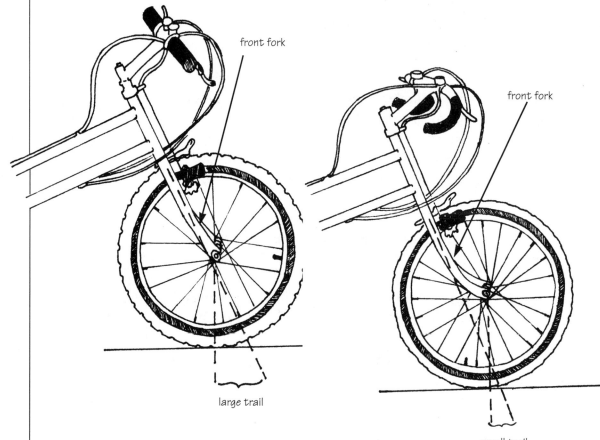

front fork

front fork

large trail

small trail

There is one more thing that makes a bicycle easy to ride. When you feel as though you are going to tip over, you react instinctively by turning the front wheel in the direction of the fall. Instead of tipping over, the bicycle now travels in a curved path. The tilt of the bicycle begins a process that creates the centripetal force needed for the turn. Thus, turning the bicycle in the direction of the fall restabilizes the bicycle and you can get back onto your original path by shifting your weight and steering the wheel in the direction you want to go.

ACTIVITY 2

GEARING UP

What do the gears do for your bicycle? If your bicycle
has gears on it, go for a ride and try different gears as
you are pedaling.

Procedure

1. On level ground, start first in a low gear and then
   in a higher gear. What is the difference?
2. On level ground, pedal as fast as you can in
   a low gear and then in a higher gear. What is
   the difference?
3. On a steep hill, pedal in a low gear and then in
   a higher gear. What is the difference?

ACTIVITY 3

MORE GEARING UP

Turn your bicycle upside down so that it rests on its
handlebars and seat. Place a piece of white tape on the
rear tire as a marker.

tape

Procedure

1. Put the bicycle in a low gear. Count the number of gear teeth on the front sprocket and on the back sprocket for the gear that you are using.

2. Put the bicycle in a high gear. Again count the number of gear teeth on the front sprocket and on the back sprocket for the gear that you are using.

3. Using your hand, put a small amount of resistance on the back tire. Turn the pedal crank one complete turn while you observe the back wheel. How many turns does the back wheel make in one complete pedal crank?

How does this activity relate to what you observed in the previous activity when you were riding your bike?

Explanation

The way that the gears and chain work on a bicycle depends entirely on the sizes of the two sprockets and, in this case, the number of teeth each gear has. In any pair of gears, the larger gear will rotate more slowly than the smaller gear, but it will rotate with greater force. The bigger the difference in size between the two gears, the bigger the difference in speed and force.

The different gear sizes allow you to strike a balance between force and distance. In low gears the ratio of front sprocket teeth to back sprocket teeth allows the rear tire to turn fewer times for one pedal turn than in higher gears. But you need less force to make the turn. This is helpful on hills, where you may find it difficult to ride in higher gears. On the other hand, in higher gears the ratio of front sprocket teeth to back sprocket teeth allows the rear tire to turn more times for one pedal turn than in lower gears. This makes it easier for you to reach higher speeds on level ground in higher gears.

TAKE OFF
FLYING OBJECTS

People have long been fascinated by flying objects and have wanted to fly. Kites marked the beginning of our quest to overcome earth's gravity.

Kites have been flown in China for over 3,000 years. They have also been used in a number of scientific endeavors. In 1752, Benjamin Franklin used a kite to conduct electricity from lightning down a wet cord to a key. In 1847 a kite was used to pull a cable across the Niagara River between the United States and Canada to form a link in the river's first suspension bridge. Alexander Graham Bell even developed huge tetrahedral box kites that were capable of carrying people.

But it was the Wright brothers' airplane, in 1903 at Kitty Hawk, North Carolina, that finally made people capable of flight.

ACTIVITY 1
PAPER PLANES

Paper planes can teach you a great deal about **aerodynamics,** the study of the forces that act on an object as it moves through the air. A number of aerodynamic forces keep any plane in the air. Make some paper planes and see for yourself how these forces work.

Procedure

1. Use your own design to make an airplane out of an $8^1/_2 \times 11$–inch (22×28–cm) piece of paper.

2 Test your design by launching it with minimal effort from a fixed height. Launch it with only a wrist flick from, say, 3 feet (1 m) off the ground.

3 Measure the distance from the starting point to where the plane first hit the ground.

4 Record your results and repeat the procedure several more times.

5 For each flight, divide the distance the plane traveled by the height from where it started. The result is the lift/drag (L/D) ratio, as explained shortly

6 Design another plane and compare the results. Repeat the entire experiment again. See if you can improve your design and get a higher L/D ratio.

◆ MORE FUN STUFF TO DO ◆

Flying Higher

Repeat the procedure, but this time use the same design with different materials. Try tissue paper, newspaper, heavy construction paper, and other kinds of paper. Can you come up with a better design than the one you made in the previous activity? Have a contest with your friends: Who can design a paper airplane that will stay in the air the longest? Or travel the farthest?

Explanation

According to Bernoulli's principle, air moves faster across the top surface of an airplane wing, creating a lower air pressure that pulls the wing up. This effect is called **lift**. If lift is greater than the force of gravity, the plane should stay aloft. **Drag**, on the other hand, is a retarding force produced by air resistance that causes an airplane to slow down and thus decreases lift.

The **lift/drag ratio** is a proportion of the distance that a plane, without power, will travel horizontally as it loses height vertically. The higher the L/D ratio, the farther a plane will glide after it loses power. For example, an average single-engine airplane can glide 10,000 feet (3,670 m) as it descends 1,000 feet (367 m). This is an L/D ratio of 10:1. A fighter jet may have a lower ratio, while a sail plane or glider will have a much higher ratio.

✦ ACTIVITY 2
FLYING CIRCLES

Not all wings look like the ones you usually see on an airplane. Try making a paper plane with circular wings.

Procedure

1. Cut two strips of paper, making the first strip $1/2 \times 3^1/_4$ inches (1.5 × 9 cm) and the second strip $3/4 \times 4^3/_4$ inches (2 × 12 cm).

2. Make a loop out of each strip of paper, overlapping the ends. Tape the ends inside and outside the loop so that the overlapping area will form a narrow slit.

3. Insert the ends of a regular-sized plastic straw into the slits and tape the straw in place.

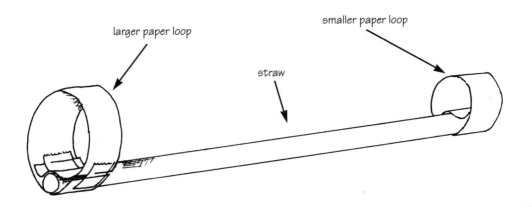

larger paper loop

smaller paper loop

straw

4 Experiment with your new airplane. Does it fly better with the larger loop in the front or in the back?

5 Try making different-sized loops. Does the plane fly better with a different design? Will it fly if one loop is on the top of the straw and the other is on the bottom?

Explanation

The flying circles create lift in the same way as an airplane wing. Faster moving air on the top of the circles creates a lower pressure and thus lift. This helps keep the flying machine in the air even if it doesn't look like a normal airplane.

■ ACTIVITY 3

THE HELICOPTER

This paper model will autorotate on its trip to the ground.

Procedure

1 Trace the helicopter pattern illustrated on the facing page.

2 Cut your tracing along all solid lines. Fold along all dotted lines as follows.

3 Fold "A" and "B" inward.

4 Fold "C" upward.

5 Fold "D" forward, and fold "E" backward. "D" and "E" are the floppy rotors. Your helicopter should look like the small picture on the facing page.

Helicopter Pattern

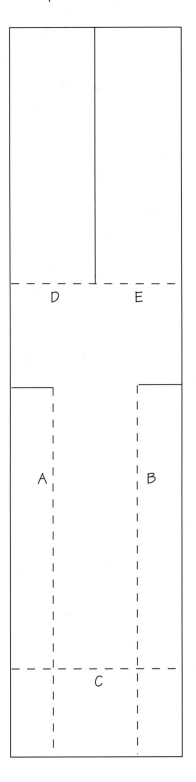

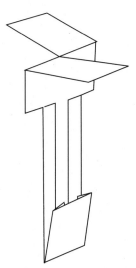

6. Hold the helicopter so that the floppy rotors are on top and drop it from a high place.

7. Drop the helicopter a few more times. Do the floppy rotors always turn in the same direction?

8. Put a paper clip over the folded part at "C." Does this change the flight pattern?

9. Modify the design and test the new model. For example, make longer rotors or use other materials, such as cardboard. Which material flies the best?

Explanation

As the "helicopter" falls, air hits the floppy rotors. Since the rotors are on opposite sides of the helicopter and offset from center, the air hitting the rotors causes the helicopter to spin. This slows its fall to earth. This spinning is similar to what happens to maple and sycamore tree seeds as they fall. Some of the factors that affect tree seeds in their journey—weight, surface area, shape—also affect real helicopters and other flying machines.

TOYS
HOW DO THEY DO THAT?

Have you ever wondered who designs toys? Do toymakers go to college and get a degree in "toy design"? Not exactly, but a good deal of science and engineering go into making toys. Many toys operate the way they do because of some very basic science.

In this section, you will investigate the science involved in the design of selected toys. Try the following activities and see if you can figure out the scientific principles behind them.

ACTIVITY 1

JUMPING ANIMALS

A pop-over mouse or kangaroo is an unusual device. It's a windup toy that will jump up in the air and do a flip, landing on its feet.

Procedure

1. Wind up the toy and set it on a flat surface. Watch it flip. How does it land? Does it flip the same way every time?
2. Put it on an angle and watch it flip. What happens that is different?
3. Put it on a soft surface like a pillow and watch it flip. What happens?
4. Why is the tail an important part of the design?
5. Put miniature marshmallows on the ears of the animal and then watch it flip. How are these flips different?

Explanation

Most windup jumping animals have a spring inside them with drive gears that cause the animal to lean forward during the early stage of motion. After the animal leans forward, the spring causes the legs to "jump" or move quickly. This throws the animal up and back into a perfect back somersault, landing the animal on its feet.

The tail increases landing stability. Flipping the animal off a soft surface (such as a pillow) or changing the weight distribution (by adding marshmallows) decreases stability and changes the somersault action so that the animal will not land on its feet.

⬛ ACTIVITY 2

STRING IT ALONG—YO-YO

Why does the yo-yo climb back up its string?

Procedure

1. Watch the yo-yo as it moves down and up on its string. How does it move?
2. Relax your hand when the yo-yo reaches the end of its string. What does the yo-yo do?
3. Throw the yo-yo upward rather than downward to start it. What happens?

Explanation

The yo-yo works, in part, because its spinning causes a gyroscopic stability (see Activity 1 in "Go for a Ride: The Bicycle," page 70, and Activity 4 in this section for more information about the gyroscope). The spinning yo-yo will maintain its circular motion unless some outside force (such as a poor yo-yoer) acts on it.

When the yo-yo is in your hand, it has potential, or stored, energy. As you let it unwind down the string, some of that potential energy is converted into kinetic energy and the yo-yo spins faster. At the bottom of the string, all the potential energy has been turned into kinetic energy and the yo-yo, spinning very fast, has enough energy to rewind itself.

If you relax your hand when the yo-yo reaches the end of the string, you can make the yo-yo "sleep" or spin freely. This is because the lack of hand motion decreases the friction between the yo-yo and the string so that the yo-yo can't rewind.

 ## ACTIVITY 3

STRETCH IT—SLINKY™

A Slinky spring toy is a coil of flat wire or plastic that is wound up to make a spring. It can teach you a lot about waves.

Procedure

1. Stretch out the Slinky on a smooth floor. This works best if you stretch it out between two people. Move one end of the Slinky from side to side quickly while your partner holds the other end. What happens? Does the wave that you have made stop when it reaches the other person?

2. Move the Slinky forward (toward the other person) and back, and watch what happens. How are these waves different from the wave you made in step 1?

3. Create waves again as you did in step 1. Make the waves go faster and faster. What happens? Can you make the waves go just fast enough that the waves seem to stop?

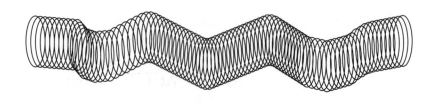

Explanation

The Slinky's ability to bounce back is due to the elastic quality of the plastic or metal that it's made from. Thus, when you created waves, the Slinky bounced back to its original position.

In step 1 of the activity, you created a **transverse wave**, a wave that moves perpendicular to its source (in this case, you). In step 2 you created a **compression wave**, a wave that moves in the same direction as its source. If you didn't move the Slinky too fast, the waves appeared to be moving away from you. When you moved the Slinky faster in step 3, you created a **standing wave**, a wave in which the movement occurs at regular intervals so that segments of the Slinky actually stand still. Where the Slinky stood still, the waves going out were met by waves coming back (as the Slinky bounced back to its original position), and the waves canceled each other out.

ACTIVITY 4

SPIN IT—GYROSCOPE

When spinning, this toy has great stability. Can you figure out why?

Procedure

1. Start a gyroscope (or a top) spinning. (You could also spin a jack on one of its points.)
2. Carefully observe the object. What happens as the spinning slows down?

Magic with a Basketball

Try to balance a basketball on your finger. What happens? Then try to spin the ball and balance it on your finger. Can you do it? With a little practice, you should be able to.

3 When it is spinning very fast, try to make it tilt. What happens? Is it easy to make it tilt?

4 Try balancing the spinning object on your finger. What happens?

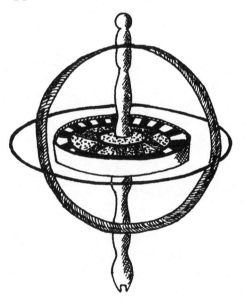

Explanation

The gyroscope is stable because of its pattern of rotation, which causes **angular momentum.** This variation on Newton's first law of motion is the tendency of a rotating object to continue rotating until acted on by an outside force. In the case of the gyroscope, the outside forces are usually friction, which slows it down, and gravity, which causes it to begin to tip over and draw circles rather than stay upright.

◈ ACTIVITY 5

SMACK IT—PADDLEBALL

A paddleball is a rubber ball attached by a rubber cord to a wooden or plastic paddle. The object of the game of paddleball is to continuously hit the ball as the rubber cord makes the ball spring back to the paddle.

Procedure

1. Try to paddle the ball downward, then sideways, and finally upward. Which way is easiest?
2. Hit the ball hard, then hit the ball softly. Which way works better?
3. What makes this toy difficult to use?

Explanation

The paddleball works because of the elastic quality of rubber. When you hit the ball and it moves away from you, the rubber cord attached to the ball stretches until it

◈ MORE FUN STUFF TO DO ◈

New Tricks for Old Toys

Besides these toys, try other ones that you may have. Try a windup car, magnetic marble, or a game of jacks. Make up your own experiments. Be a toy scientist, and see if you can learn how each toy works.

cannot stretch any farther and the ball stops. Then, as the rubber cord returns to its original shape and position, it pulls the ball back toward you.

OUT OF THIS WORLD: TOYS IN SPACE

If you have investigated the toys in this section, then you know that there is science behind the operation of each. How do you think they would work in the microgravity of a space shuttle in orbits around the earth? Dr. Carolyn Sumners, Director of Astronomy and Physics at the Houston Museum of Natural Sciences, wanted to find out the answer to that question, so she convinced NASA to send 20 dollars' worth of toys into space.

On April 12, 1985, the space shuttle *Discovery* transported 11 toys into the weightless environment of space. The five astronauts and one U.S. senator on board spent several hours "testing" the toys to better understand the effects of gravity's pull on them.

A videotape of the toy experiments was made in which the astronauts demonstrated how the toys work both on earth and in space. Freed from earth's gravity, the toys worked remarkably well. Several worked better in the microgravity environment. The yo-yo was able to move in all directions, up or down, equally well. The paddleball showed similar characteristics—I think that even I could play with that toy in the shuttle.

If you want to learn more about how the toys operated in space, the videotape can be purchased for $29.50 (plus $3 shipping and handling) from: Sopris West Inc., 1140 Boston Avenue, Longmont, Colorado 80501.

4 Excitement on the Midway

Fun Foods and Games of Chance

Rides and toys aren't the only places to look for science at the amusement park. You can learn about chemistry by studying popcorn and hot dogs. Watch a game of chance and you may be able to figure out how you can win at it (or why an amusement park can never lose), because mathematics can help explain the rules of chance and predict what will happen next.

⬛ IT'S EXPLOSIVE
POPCORN

Have you ever wondered about popcorn—not why
it tastes so good at an amusement park, but why it pops
at all? Try the following investigation and see what
you can learn about this great food.

⬛ ACTIVITY

POP GOES THE KERNEL

Procedure

1. Take a jar or bag of uncooked popcorn. Look at
   the kernels. How many are there in the bag? Is it
   in the hundreds or thousands?

2. Measure out a certain amount, say $1/4$ cup (65 ml).
   Estimate how many kernels you think there are.
   Next, count the kernels. Was your estimate close to
   the actual amount?

3. Now, ask an adult to cut a kernel in half. Examine
   the kernel. What does the way it is made tell you
   about it?

4. Pop the corn in the usual way, then look at the
   popped kernels. Do they look similar or is each one
   different?

5. Compare a popped kernel to the one you cut in half.
   How are they similar? Can you find the white part
   in the kernel and the kernel in the popped corn?

Explanation

Popcorn pops because of the water that is contained
inside each kernel. Popcorn is approximately 20% water.
When the kernel is heated, the water is also heated and

changes to steam. This change creates great pressure inside the kernel. The kernel has a tough outer covering that can initially hold the pressure. But when the pressure of the water gets too great, the outer covering breaks and the corn pops.

Because the outer covering tends to break in a similar way for most kernels, all popped kernels usually look pretty much alike unless they crumble in the popping process. A popped kernel will be 25 to 30 times larger than an unpopped kernel.

Corn isn't the only thing that will pop. Several breakfast cereals are made in a similar way. Both rice and wheat can be "popped" into puffed rice (like Rice Krispies®) or puffed wheat.

THE HOT DOG
ENJOY IT WITH RELISH

Although its forerunners are the sausages made in Germany and elsewhere in Europe, the hot dog originated in North America, first appearing at the amusement park at Coney Island. Food has always been a part of the amusement park experience, so it stands to reason that the traditional hot dog with relish and mustard should begin there. Coney Island was a proving ground for many innovations. Roller coasters started there, the famous magician Harry Houdini learned his trade there, and the British novelist Charles Dickens claimed it was the only place he liked in America.

But what about the hot dog itself? What's in it? What can science tell us? Experiment with a hot dog, and maybe you can eat it afterward.

ACTIVITY
SOLAR HOT DOG COOKER

Hot dogs can be boiled, fried, roasted, or cooked in almost any way imaginable. Watch hot dogs being cooked at an amusement park, or cook them yourself at home—but this experiment will work only on a hot, sunny day.

Procedure

1. Cover one side of a piece of cardboard that is about 12 × 18 inches (30 × 45 cm) with aluminum foil.

2 Bend the cardboard into a half cylinder so that the foil is on the inside. Wrap a large rubber band or string around each end to hold the cardboard in this shape.

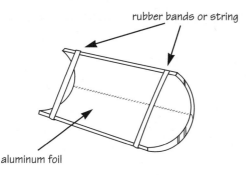

rubber bands or string

aluminum foil

3 Cut a box whose long side is slightly shorter than the half cylinder's long side, as shown, to make a holder for the cardboard half cylinder.

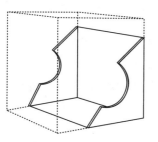

4 Position the cardboard half cylinder in the curve you've cut in the box. This is your solar hot dog cooker.

5 Ask an adult to cut the hook of a coat hanger as shown and bend the hanger to make a holder for the hot dog.

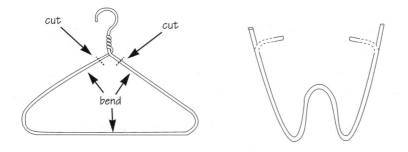

cut   cut

bend

4 | Wash the holder, then attach the hot dog to the two open ends.

5 | Place your solar hot dog cooker so that it directly faces the sun. Position the holder so that the hot dog is horizontally right in the middle of the cooker.

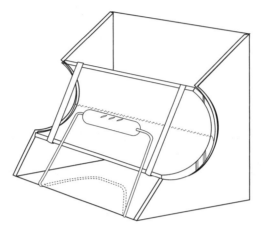

6 | Watch the hot dog while it cooks. Does it get bigger (go "plump")?

7 | It may take a while, but the hot dog should cook. When it's done, eat and enjoy!

Explanation

The foil, bent in a half cylinder, reflects the light and heat from the sun toward the center of the cooker. This concentrates, or focuses, a lot of energy at one place. That energy is enough to cook your hot dog.

As hot dogs cook, they usually get slightly larger. That's because as any matter (in this case, food) heats up, the atoms and molecules in the food start to move faster and farther apart. This makes the hot dog get slightly larger. Hot dogs usually give off juices while they cook as well. These juices are the fats in the hot dog meat that melt when they are heated.

FEATHER LIGHT
COTTON CANDY

Have you ever wondered how cotton candy is made?
I'm sure you can tell by the taste what's in it. If you
guessed sugar, you're right! That's all it is. Next time
you go to an amusement park, watch while they make
cotton candy.

ACTIVITY
SPUN SWEETNESS

Ask yourself the following questions while you watch
the cotton candy being made.

Procedure

1. Where does the raw sugar go in?
2. Where does the "cotton candy" come out?
3. How does color get added?
4. How is the paper cone held to collect the cotton
   candy?
5. Put a piece of cotton candy in your mouth. Let it sit
   on your tongue without eating it. What happens?

Explanation

The cotton candy maker takes sugar and heats it in
a spinning tube. As the sugar melts, the spinning causes
the liquid sugar to be drawn out into long, thin strands.
As these strands come out of the spinning tube, they
stick to the paper cone. The candy maker twirls the
cone around so that the sugar sticks to the cone in
the shape of a ball.

GAMES OF CHANCE
THE MATHEMATICS OF WINNING

Have you ever wondered if the games at amusement parks are rigged? Why is it that you can never seem to win that stuffed animal that you want? And when you do, it seems as though you had to play all afternoon. The answer is in mathematics and the laws of probability. Play the following games and see if you can figure out how they work.

ACTIVITY

"LUCKY" DICE

Procedure

1. Take 30 pennies and one die (one of a pair of dice).
2. Put 15 of the pennies in a pile for the "amusement park" and keep 15 pennies for yourself.
3. Bet 1 penny that you can guess what number will come up next on the die. If you guess correctly, the amusement park will pay you 4 cents. If you are wrong, the amusement park will keep your penny.
4. Play the game for 10 rolls of the die.
5. Total the amount of money you have and the amount that the amusement park has at the end of 10 rolls. Who won more money?
6. Try the game again to see if your luck changes.

Explanation

The "amusement park" will always win this game in the long run. Although it sounds like a good deal to win 4 cents when you bet only 1 cent, it is really a sucker's game.

The mathematics works like this. The die has six sides. This means that on any particular throw of the die, you have a one-in-six chance of guessing correctly. (For this number to prove true, you would have to roll the die a great number of times. Sometimes you will do better than these odds, and sometimes you will do worse.)

However, even though the die gives you a one-in-six chance, the amusement park only pays you as if the odds were one in four (your 4-cent winning prize). Because you are paid less than the chance given by the die, the amusement park will always win in the long run.

With other games, such as throwing darts or knocking milk bottles off a shelf, the mathematics is similar. You may get lucky and win on your first turn. But usually it takes more turns to win than what the prize is worth. You are paid less than the chance of winning.

WHERE'S THE WATER?
DIAPERS AND SLEIGHT OF HAND

ACTIVITY 1
KEEPING BABY DRY

Procedure

1. Spread a sheet of newspaper on the kitchen table.
2. Take a disposable diaper and cut it in half with a pair of scissors so that you can see what is inside it.
3. How many layers are there? Are they made of different materials? Can you tell just by looking what each material is used for?
4. Take apart the middle layer of cotton. Examine it closely. What do you see? How is it made?
5. Take the cotton layer and shake it vigorously back and forth. You may need to rub it as well. What happens? Did you find anything that might make the diapers work better?
6. Small particles should have come out of the cotton layer. Take a few of the particles and put them in a cup. Add a few drops of water. What happens?
7. Take a few more particles and try the next activity.

ACTIVITY 2
THE THREE-CUP MONTE

This is a variation of an old carnival game. In the original game, a pea is placed under one of three walnut shells. After the shells are quickly moved around, the player tries to guess which shell has the pea. In the following game, your friends try to guess which cup has the water.

Procedure

1. Place the particles you saved from the previous activity into one of three identical cups.

2. Get a group of friends together and tell them you are going to make some water disappear. Quickly show them that the cups are empty. *Quickly* is the key word. You don't want to let them see the particles.

3. Pour a small amount of water into one of the empty cups. Switch the cups around quickly and ask your friends to guess which cup has the water. They should be able to find it because the cups are right side up.

4. Tell them they are correct and pour the water into the cup with the particles. Again switch the cups around quickly. Ask which cup has the water.

5. This time when they answer correctly, turn the cup upside down. The water should remain stuck in the cup when you do this. The water has seemingly disappeared.

6. Take your bows.

Explanation

There are certain polymers (long molecules) that have a strong **hygroscopic** nature. This means that they are capable of absorbing and holding moisture. Some polymers can absorb and hold over 50 times their weight in water. One common molecule of this type is called polysodium acrylate and can be purchased from magic stores under the name Water Slush™. This type of polymer has been added to diapers to hold moisture and help keep baby dry.

BUCKET BALL

IF AT FIRST YOU DON'T SUCCEED

When you look at some amusement park games, they seem so easy. Then why is it so difficult to win the big prize? Is it true that practice makes perfect?

ACTIVITY

PRACTICE MAKES PERFECT

Procedure

1. Find a wastebasket and a tennis ball.
2. Place the wastebasket on the floor and stand about 6 feet (2 m) away with the tennis ball.
3. Throw the ball underhand and try to make it land in the wastebasket. Keep trying until you get it in. How many times did it take you to make it?
4. Now stand 10 feet (3 m) away and try to make the ball land in the wastebasket again. Keep trying until you get it in. How many times did it take you this time?

Explanation

There is a certain amount of skill involved in many amusement park games. If you practice enough, you can win the prize. But how many times do you have to practice to get good enough at the game to win? If it had cost you 25 cents each time you threw the tennis ball, how much would you have spent by the time you got it in the wastebasket? By the time you've practiced an amusement park game enough to win, it's cost you more than the prize is worth. While practice may make perfect, in many amusement park games practice can also make you penniless.

Skittles

Skittles is an old carnival sideshow game that is still played in some amusement parks. It look impossible to win because it involves hitting a bottle with a ball that is attached to a pendulum suspended directly above the bottle, as shown.

pendulum suspended directly above the bottle

Can you make the ball hit the bottle on the return swing?

To win the prize, the player must start the pendulum so that it misses the bottle on the forward swing and hits it on the return swing. The player is not allowed to throw the pendulum over the bottle. It seems like a simple trick. After a few tries to find the right pendulum swing, it should be possible to clean out the show. Set it up for yourself and try it.

(continued)

Explanation

Because the ball is attached to a string, the ball moves around the bottle in a circle and continues moving in that circle until acted on by an outside force. This movement is due to a law of physics called the conservation of angular momentum, which states that **angular momentum** cannot be created or destroyed. (See Activity 4, "Spin It—Gyroscope," on page 84 if you need a reminder about angular momentum.)

However, there is one sneaky way to hit the bottle. Twist the string so that on the throw, the ball spins (creating an outside force). This creates a situation similar to that of throwing a curveball. Rather than orbit around the bottle, the ball can now hit it.

GLOSSARY

aerodynamics   The study of the forces that act on an object as it moves through the air.

angular momentum   The tendency of a rotating object to continue rotating until acted on by an outside force.

Bernoulli's principle   When any fluid, such as air, flows, its pressure decreases when its speed increases. Very important when you fly a plane, sail a boat, or throw a curveball.

center of mass   The point in an object where its mass is equal in all directions. Objects that spin rotate around that point.

centripetal force   The force that causes an object to move in a circle. It literally means the "center seeking" force.

circle of least confusion   The area where a blurred image hits the retina.

clothoid loop   A teardrop shape used extensively in the design of looping roller coasters.

compression wave A wave that moves in the same direction as its source.

conservation of angular momentum Angular momentum cannot be created or destroyed.

drag A retarding force produced by air resistance that causes an airplane to slow down and thus decreases lift.

elastic The ability of an object to return to its original shape after being deformed. Rubber balls and bubbles have this property.

friction A force that works in an opposite direction to an object that is moving along a surface.

fulcrum The support about which a lever turns.

hemisphere Half of a sphere. A sphere is any object shaped like a ball.

hygroscopic Capable of absorbing and holding moisture.

impulse The product of a force and the time interval over which it acts.

kinetic energy Energy that is being used, the energy caused by motion.

law of conservation of energy Energy can change from one form to another but cannot be created or destroyed.

lever A rigid bar used to support a weight. When used with a fulcrum, the lever becomes a simple machine.

lift The effect of air as it moves across the upper surface of an airplane wing or other similar shape, creating a lower pressure that pulls the wing up.

lift/drag ratio   A proportion of the distance that a plane, without power, will travel horizontally as it loses height vertically.

mass   Properties that cause an object to have weight due to gravity.

microgravity   A gravitational force that is less than the force of gravity at the surface of the earth. Astronauts experience microgravity when they are in orbit around the earth.

momentum   The product of the mass and the velocity of an object.

Newton's three laws of motion   (1) An object moving in a straight line will keep moving in that direction unless acted on by an outside force; (2) If an object is moved by a force, it will move in the direction of the force; (3) For every action there is an equal and opposite reaction.

parabola   A mathematical shape that is similar to a section of a circle in which the ends have been straightened. It is the path a thrown object takes due to gravity's pull.

pendulum   A simple device in which an object is suspended by rope, chain, or string from a central pivot point.

period   The time needed for a pendulum to complete one cycle of motion.

point retinal image   An image that is in focus at one point on the retina.

potential energy   Energy that is stored for later use.

sphere   A ball-like shape that has maximum volume and minimum surface area.

standing wave   A wave in which the movement occurs at regular intervals so that segments stand still.

surface tension   The force of attraction between water molecules that creates a "thin skin" on the surface of the water.

transverse wave   A wave that moves perpendicular to its source.

variable   Any factor that changes in an experiment.

velocity   Speed in a specific direction.

weight   The force with which an object is pulled toward the earth by gravity.

BIBLIOGRAPHY

Brancazio, Peter. *Sport Science*. New York: Simon & Schuster, 1984.

Cartmell, Robert. *The Incredible Scream Machine*: *A History of the Roller Coaster*. Bowling Green: Bowling Green State University Popular Press, 1987.

Ingram, Jay. *Real Live Science*. Toronto: Green de Pencier Books, 1992.

Morris, Campbell. *Advanced Paper Aircraft Construction Mk III*. London: Angus & Robertson Publishers, 1987.

Schrier, Eric, and William Allman, Editors. *Newton at the Bat: The Science in Sports*. New York: Charles Scribner's Sons, 1988.

Walker, Jearl. "The Amateur Scientist," *Scientific American*. Vol. 249, No. 4 (October 1983), pp. 162–169.

Wiese, James. *Amusement Park Physics*. Franklin Park: Central Scientific Company, 1989.

INDEX

Moisture. *See* Water
Molecules, 94, 100
Momentum, 53
Morrison, Fred, 68
Motion
  and Bernoulli's principle,
    60, 61
  Newton's three laws of,
    21-22, 45, 47-48
Music Machine (ride), 47-
  48

Nature treasure hunt, 31-33
Needles, tree, finding and
  classifying, 31-33
Newton, Sir Isaac, 21
Newton's three laws of
  motion
  and bumper cars, 53
  and centripetal force, 22,
    45, 47-48
  explained, 21-22
  and merry-go-rounds, 22
  variations on, 71, 85

Paddleball, 86-87
Paper planes, 75-80
Parabola, 16, 65, 66
Pendulum
  experiments with, 7-9, 10,
    11, 12-16
  explained, 7
  how to make, 11
  period of, 7, 8, 9-10, 14-
    15, 16
  principles of, 9-10, 13
  and Skittles game, 101-2
  and swings, 7-10, 101-2
Pitcher, baseball, 62-64
Planes, paper, 75-80
Plasterer, Eiffel, 30
Playgrounds, 1-33
  bubble blowing, 27-30

g force measurements, 23-
  26
merry-go-round, 19-22,
  25, 26
nature treasure hunt, 31-33
seesaw, 17-18
slide, 2-6
swing, 7-10, 26
Point retinal image, 55
Polymers, 99
Polysodium acrylate, 99
Popcorn, 90-91
Potential energy
  explained, 4
  and roller coasters, 40, 41
  and slides, 4, 5
  and swings, 10
  and yo-yos, 83
Probability, laws of, 96
Pumping swings, 10-11

Retina, 55
Roller coasters, 38-44
  experiments with, 38, 39,
    42
  history of, 36-37, 44
  how to make, 39
  looping, 42-44
  principles of, 38, 40-41,
    43-44
Rotating platforms, 51
Rotation
  and angular momentum,
    85, 102
  axes of, 46-47
  gyroscopic pattern of, 71,
    85
  and Newton's three laws of
    motion, 21-22

Scrambler (ride), 46-48
Second law of motion, 22,
  48